STEVEN R. HARMON

Encountering
POPE LEO XIV

Baptist Reflections
on the Beginning of a Pontificate

© 2025
Published in the United States by Nurturing Faith, Macon, GA.
Nurturing Faith is a book imprint of Good Faith Media (goodfaithmedia.org).
Library of Congress Cataloging-in-Publication Data is available.

ISBN: 978-1-63528-270-2

All rights reserved. Printed in the United States of America.

"How fascinating to read a Baptist's take on one of the most Catholic of all institutions: the papacy. Professor Harmon's warm, inviting, and engaging book is a window not only into the exciting election of Pope Leo XIV, but also Catholicism and, more broadly, Christianity. I'm grateful for Harmon's unique perspective, his insightful comments, and his desire to help others understand more about our shared faith."

—Fr. James Martin, S.J., *America* magazine editor at large, consultor for the Vatican's Dicastery for Communication, and author of *Learning to Pray: A Guide for Everyone*

"Harmon combines his roles as on-the-ground journalist at the recent historical conclave, expert Baptist theologian, and seasoned international ecumenical participant to offer an insightful analysis of Pope Leo XIV. The result is a compelling account of why Baptists and indeed all Christians might discover in the new pope a resource for renewal and unity."

—Elizabeth Newman, Adjunct Professor of Theology at Duke Divinity School and Union Presbyterian Seminary, co-chair of the joint commission for the Baptist-Catholic dialogue (Phase III), and former chair of the Baptist World Alliance Commission on Baptist Doctrine and Christian Unity

"Closely-studied and timely…Harmon's reporting of the election of Pope Leo XIV evokes the people-filled piazzas and laneways of Rome and invites his readers to consider the significance of the pontificate of the first U.S.-born pope. His honest assessment of responses by Baptists to the death of Leo's predecessor, Pope Francis, as well as to the election of this new pope is invaluable…an essential resource for students of Baptist ecumenical engagement."

—Darrell Jackson, Principal, Whitley College, University of Divinity, Melbourne, Australia and chair of the Baptist World Alliance Commission on Baptist Doctrine and Christian Unity

*In memory of
Claude Upshaw Broach
(1913–1997)*

Contents

Acknowledgements 1

Chapters

1: The Theologian Who Became Pope................................... 3

2: The People's Pope 9

3: Arriving in Rome 21

4: Anticipating the Conclave... 29

5: Who Might Become Pope?... 39

6: Conclave Day One... 49

7: Conclave Day Two: White Smoke!.................................. 59

8: Early Answers to Pre-Conclave Questions 69

9: Pope Leo XIV's First Weekend 77

10: A Theology for Journalists (and Everyone Who Uses Words) 89

11: Baptists and the Pope 97

12: What's Ahead for Leo XIV's Pontificate? 107

13: A Prayer for Pope Leo XIV.. 121

Acknowledgements

I am grateful to the leadership and staff of Good Faith Media for their generous support of the project that became this book. Good Faith Media CEO Mitch Randall enthusiastically embraced what I proposed to him and secured the funding that took me to Rome as a special correspondent to cover the conclave that elected Pope Leo XIV. Craig Nash, Starlette Thomas, Cliff Vaughn, Cally Chisholm, Roderious Phillips, and Missy Randall each provided indispensable help with logistics and the production of my dispatches from Rome. Starlette and Craig in particular supplied editorial fine-tuning of my writing that is reflected in the adaptation of that material in portions of this book.

I'm grateful also to the Nurturing Faith Book Acquisitions Team for their interest in publishing *Encountering Pope Leo XIV* and in particular to Nurturing Faith Books author liaison Carol Brown for her guidance and assistance in moving my manuscript toward publication.

While my wife Kheresa and son Timothy were not able to travel with me to Rome, they were excited about my opportunity to do so and strengthened me through their encouragement, support, and love. Their participation in my experiences in Rome through text messages, phone calls, and FaceTime video connections are memories of this time that I will always cherish.

My students and colleagues at Gardner-Webb University School of Divinity were likewise excited for me and were supportive and understanding as I made various adjustments to bring my teaching semester to an early conclusion so I could travel to Rome for the conclave. My School of Divinity and the university to which it belongs have helped me flourish as a

Baptist ecumenical theologian, and my students and colleagues there have made their own significant contributions to the expression of that vocation that is reflected in this book.

I have much gratitude for the support and encouragement given to me in my work in Rome and in the writing and publication of this book by the members and ministers of my local church community, St. John's Baptist Church in Charlotte, North Carolina. I am especially grateful to the diaconate and Missions Resource Team of St. John's Baptist Church for their generous contribution of a sponsoring gift from the congregation to Good Faith Media that assisted with the costs of publication. This book is dedicated to the memory of their longtime pastor Claude Upshaw Broach (1913–1997), who served as pastor of St. John's Baptist Church from 1944 until his retirement in 1974. A portion of Chapter 3 of this book tells more fully the story of how Dr. Broach, dismayed that both the Baptist World Alliance and the Southern Baptist Convention to which the congregation then belonged had declined the opportunity to send official ecumenical observers to the Second Vatican Council, ended up with an invitation to travel to Rome himself as an accredited "Visiting Theologian" and observed the final ten days of the Council, November 29 through December 8, 1965. I went to Rome with the sense of following in our respected former pastor's steps of constructive Baptist ecumenical engagement with Catholic Christianity.

Steven R. Harmon
The Season after Pentecost, 2025

Chapter 1
The Theologian Who Became Pope

For both Pope Leo XIV and me, the story recounted in this book began long before the conclave that elected Robert Francis Prevost as the 267th pope of the Catholic Church on May 8, 2025.

For me, there's a sense in which it began in first grade in Rotan, Texas. One of my classmates would cross himself before eating his lunch in the cafeteria each day. "That's what we do in my church," he explained to me. That wasn't something people did in the Baptist church my family attended. "Freddy's very religious," I remember telling my mother when she joined me for lunch one day and my classmate repeated the ritual sitting across the table from us. That is my earliest conscious memory of Catholic faith and practice, and I suppose it was also my first awareness that there were Christians who were not like Baptists.

Later my family moved to Rosebud, Texas, where some of my high school classmates were from the nearby town of Westphalia, which had been founded in the late nineteenth century by German Catholic immigrants from the region of the same name. My Westphalia classmates were members of the Church of the Visitation, which from its construction in 1894 until the original structure was destroyed by fire in 2019 was the largest wooden church building west of the Mississippi River. They attended a parochial school with nuns from a local convent as their teachers through the eighth grade and then enrolled with us at Rosebud-Lott High School. From these friends and a number of Hispanic friends who were members of a Catholic parish in Rosebud, I learned much about this different approach to following and worshiping the God disclosed in Jesus Christ whom I and my Baptist family and friends sought to follow and worship.

I discerned a calling to vocational ministry during high school, which led to undergraduate work in the School of Christian Studies at Baptist-related Howard Payne University in Brownwood, Texas, and then graduate seminary studies at Southwestern Baptist Theological Seminary in Fort Worth, Texas. I continued to doctoral studies in theology at Southwestern that focused on patristic theology—the theology of the early church fathers (and mothers, too) from the end of the New Testament era through the next few centuries who shaped the theological heritage of the whole church, but especially of the Catholic and Eastern Orthodox churches that emphasized historical continuity with patristic Christianity. My participation in the story told in this book has particular roots in a year of my doctoral studies undertaken in the Early Christian Studies program at The Catholic University of America in Washington, D.C., where in the 1994–1995 academic year I lived in a graduate dormitory along with a number of priests who were enrolled in research graduate programs there. These studies and experiences played a role in invitations later to serve on the Baptist World Alliance delegations to joint commissions for two phases of ecumenical dialogue with the Catholic Church, 2006–2010 and 2017–2022, along with dialogues with the Anglican Communion and at a preliminary stage with the Eastern Orthodox churches.

For Pope Leo XIV, the story includes the pontificates of his predecessors Pope Benedict XVI and Pope Francis. I have had audiences with both previous popes in connection with my participation in the Baptist-Catholic dialogues. For Pope Leo XIV, for me, and for the readers of this book, encounters with his two immediate predecessors are important background for the story of the beginning of Leo's pontificate.

THE THEOLOGIAN POPE

Pope Emeritus Benedict XVI, who died on the morning of December 31, 2022, at the age of 95, leaves a legacy that will be the subject of intense discussion and debate for decades to come. In the hours that followed the news of Pope Benedict's death, I found myself thinking of him primarily as the theologian who happened to have become pope in the course of his theological career.

That's how I experienced him when the joint commission to Phase II of the international dialogue between the Baptist World Alliance and the Catholic Church, on which I served, had a private audience with Pope Benedict in December 2007. After Pope Benedict greeted us and assured us of his prayers for the progress of our dialogue and for our families in our absence, the chairs of our respective delegations communicated our greetings to him. Baptist delegation chair Paul Fiddes of the University of Oxford mentioned in his greetings that we'd found Benedict's commentary on the Vatican II Dogmatic Constitution on Divine Revelation *Dei Verbum*, which he'd written not long after the council as young theologian Joseph Ratzinger, most helpful in our discussions that week.[1] At that moment Benedict suddenly sat up straight in his chair and leaned forward with brightened eyes. In that moment he was not the pope, but a career academic theologian who'd just learned that someone was actually reading and interested in something he'd published.

Later in the audience, we were each introduced to Pope Benedict by our delegation chairs. Paul Fiddes introduced me as "a professor of theology from the United States." Benedict said, "A professor already? But you are so young!" Having turned 40 only three months earlier, I received those words gladly. (It should be noted that fifteen years later, Pope Francis did not say the same thing to me during the audience our joint commission had with him in December 2022.) Pope Benedict's words to me underscored his own ongoing identification with the role of professor of theology.

THEOLOGIAN JOSEPH RATZINGER

While Pope Benedict's ecclesiastical career included service as Archbishop of Munich and Freising (1977–1982), as head of the Congregation for the Doctrine of the Faith (1982–2005), and as pope (2005–2013), he was a professor of theology for most of his career. He served as a member of the faculty at the University of Bonn (1959–1963), the University of Münster (1963–1966), the University of Tübingen (1966–1969), where his colleagues included the reforming Catholic theologian Hans Küng and the

Protestant Reformed theologian Jürgen Moltmann, and finally the University of Regensburg (1969–1977).

During the Second Vatican Council (1962–1965), Ratzinger had served as one of the theological advisors to the bishops assembled for the council. Along with Küng, Edward Schillebeeckx, and Karl Rahner, he was viewed as one of the "reformers" whose theologies influenced the council to embrace ecumenical openness and comparatively more progressive positions on the relationship of the Catholic Church to the modern world. But his theology seemed to take a more conservative turn in the wake of his experience in Tübingen of the widespread Western European student protests of 1968.

The orthodox yet world-engaging theology expressed with clarity in books that Ratzinger published as a teaching theologian such as *Introduction to Christianity* (1968)[2] and *Eschatology: Death and Eternal Life* (1977)[3] paved the way for a pontificate that did not relinquish the role of writing theologian. His three-volume work *Jesus of Nazareth* published from 2007 through 2012 would have been received as a significant contribution to Christology even if it had not been written by a current pope.[4]

BENEDICT XVI, THE TEACHING POPE

All popes since the middle of the eighteenth century have exercised the teaching office of the pope in the form of papal encyclicals, starting with one issued by Pope Benedict XIV in 1740.[5] But Pope Benedict XVI's three encyclicals are especially rich expressions of theology. A Baptist theologian friend who shares my interest in dialogue with the Catholic tradition has remarked that the roles in which a pope has served before becoming pope shape his exercise of the papal office in important ways. That was certainly the case with Pope Benedict.

Benedict's encyclicals *Deus Caritas Est*, "On Christian Love" (2005),[6] *Spe Salvi*, "On Christian Hope" (2007),[7] and *Caritas in Veritate*, "On Integral Human Development in Charity and Truth" (2009)[8] articulate a theological framework for Christian engagement of the challenges of today's world that resists categorization as conservative or otherwise. On the one hand, no one would question its orthodoxy. On the other hand, it provides a theological basis for aspects of Catholic social teaching that some might dismiss as "woke" if they came from another source.

Pope Francis, who completed Benedict's unfinished encyclical *Lumen Fidei*, "On Faith" in 2013,[9] incorporated this theological framework into his own encyclicals *Laudato Si'*, "On Care for Our Common Home" (2015)[10] and *Fratelli Tutti*, "On Fraternity and Social Friendship" (2020).[11] They liberally quote from and reference Pope Benedict's encyclicals and apply their theology to care for creation and care for the people who inhabit it. Any differences between the theologies written by these two popes in this form are primarily in nuance rather than substance. But the nuances are important, as is a pastoral approach to their application.

While serving as head of the Congregation for the Doctrine of the Faith, the division of the Vatican curia with responsibility for maintaining the orthodoxy of Catholic faith and practice, the future Pope Benedict XVI was a trusted theological advisor to Pope John Paul II. It was widely rumored that John Paul II was contemplating promulgating as Catholic doctrine a definition of the status of Mary as "co-redemptrix," co-redeemer of humanity with Christ. (Two other Marian dogmas, the Immaculate Conception of Mary free from original sin, defined by Pope Pius IX in 1854, and the Assumption of Mary body and soul into heaven at the conclusion of her earthly life, defined by Pope Pius XII in 1950, are the only two times in history that a pope has made an *ex cathedra*—from the chair of Peter—definition of doctrine so far.) It is thought that it was then Cardinal Ratzinger who dissuaded John Paul II from promulgating such a doctrine, contending that while Karol Wojtyła could have made such a proposal as an individual Catholic theologian, he could not do so as Pope John Paul II responsible for teaching the faith to which the faithful give their consent.[12]

One could argue that while the papacy of John Paul II profited from the behind-the-scenes theological counsel of Joseph Ratzinger, the papacy of Benedict XVI suffered from the comparative lack of the instinct for public relations that had marked John Paul II's exercise of the office. It may be that decades from now, Pope Emeritus Benedict XVI will be remembered primarily as the pope who single-handedly modernized the papacy through his decision to resign from it. It remains to be seen how the handling of cases of clergy sex abuse during his tenure as archbishop and pope will be regarded. It may not be that future generations will think him as the professor of theology who became a pope.

Nevertheless, I believe that chief among his enduring contributions is his service as a *doctor ecclesiae*, a "teacher of the church." When subsequent popes, including Pope Leo XIV, teach theology through their encyclicals, exhortations, homilies, and other communications, they will be building on Benedict XVI's legacy of the pope as theologian.

NOTES

[1] Joseph Ratzinger, "Dogmatic Constitution on Divine Revelation: Chapter II, The Transmission of Divine Revelation," trans. William Glen-Doepel, in *Commentary on the Documents of Vatican II*, ed. Herbert Vorgrimler, vol. 3 (New York: Herder and Herder, 1967–1969), 181–198.

[2] Joseph Ratzinger, *Introduction to Christianity*, trans. J. R. Foster (London: Burns & Oates, 1969). Dates for Ratzinger's pre-pontificate books in parentheses in the chapter text refer to the original German publications.

[3] Joseph Ratzinger, *Eschatology: Death and Eternal Life*, 2nd ed., trans. Michael Waldstein, ed. Aidan Nichols (Washington, D.C.: The Catholic University of America Press, 1988).

[4] Pope Benedict XVI, *Jesus of Nazareth*, 3 vols., trans. Adrian Walker and Philip J. Whitmore (New York: Random House, 2007–2012).

[5] Pope Benedict XIV, *Ubi Primum* (December 3, 1740), https://www.vatican.va/content/benedictus-xiv/it/documents/enciclica--i-ubi-primum--i---3-dicembre-1740--nell--8217-ambito-.html, accessed 2 July 2025.

[6] Pope Benedict XVI, *Deus Caritas Est*, "On Christian Love" (December 25, 2005), https://www.vatican.va/content/benedict-xvi/en/encyclicals/documents/hf_ben-xvi_enc_20051225_deus-caritas-est.html, accessed 2 July 2025.

[7] Pope Benedict, XVI, *Spe Salvi*, "On Christian Hope" (November 30, 2007), https://www.vatican.va/content/benedict-xvi/en/encyclicals/documents/hf_ben-xvi_enc_20071130_spe-salvi.html, accessed 2 July 2025.

[8] Pope Benedict XVI, *Caritas in Veritate*, "On Integral Human Development in Charity and Truth" (June 29, 2009_, https://www.vatican.va/content/benedict-xvi/en/encyclicals/documents/hf_ben-xvi_enc_20090629_caritas-in-veritate.html, accessed 2 July 2025.

[9] Pope Francis, *Lumen Fidei*, "On Faith" (June 29, 2013), https://www.vatican.va/content/francesco/en/encyclicals/documents/papa-francesco_20130629_enciclica-lumen-fidei.html, accessed 2 July 2025.

[10] Pope Francis, *Laudato Si'*, "On Care for Our Common Home," May 24, 2015, https://www.vatican.va/content/francesco/en/encyclicals/documents/papa-francesco_20150524_enciclica-laudato-si.html, accessed 2 July 2025.

[11] Pope Francis, *Fratelli Tutti*, "On Fraternity and Social Friendship," October 3, 2020, https://www.vatican.va/content/francesco/en/encyclicals/documents/papa-francesco_20201003_enciclica-fratelli-tutti.html, accessed 2 July 2025.

[12] Ratzinger publicly confirmed his opposition to an official definition of Mary as co-redemptrix in Joseph Ratzinger, *God and the World: A Conversation with Peter Seewald* (San Francisco: Ignatius, 2002), 306.

Chapter 2

The People's Pope

My reflections on the papacy of Pope Francis, who died at the age of 88 at 7:35 a.m. local time in Rome on Monday, April 21, 2025—less than a day after delivering brief Easter Sunday greetings to worshipers in St. Peter's Basilica—are intertwined with experiences of prayer.

When Pope Benedict XVI announced on February 11, 2013, that he would resign the papacy effective at the end of that month, I remembered that Benedict had prayed for me—in the sense that during a private audience with joint delegations to a meeting in Rome of the ecumenical dialogue between the Baptist World Alliance and the Catholic Church in December 2007, I and my family were included in his pledge of prayer for us during his words of greeting: "Dear friends, I offer you my cordial good wishes and the assurance of my prayers for the important work which you have undertaken. Upon your conversations, and upon each of you and your loved ones, I gladly invoke the Holy Spirit's gifts of wisdom, understanding, strength, and peace."[1]

When I learned the news of Benedict's announced retirement, I remembered with gratitude my encounter with Benedict and his pledge of prayers, and I resolved to remember him and his post-pontifical ministry in prayer. I also invited others in my circles to join me in praying for the conclave of the College of Cardinal that would select his successor, whose ministry would have implications for all Christians and the world they inhabit.

The next month I delivered the Robert K. Campbell Memorial Lectures on Christian Unity sponsored by the Lehigh County Conferences of Churches at DeSales University in Center Valley, Pennsylvania.[2] My lectures were on March 12, the day the conclave began, and I began the first lecture by voicing a prayer for the conclave already underway in Rome.

I flew home the next morning, and on the drive home to Boiling Springs, North Carolina, from the airport in Charlotte later in the day, I heard on NPR the news of the billowing of white smoke in St. Peter's Square. I made it to my office at Gardner-Webb University just in time to watch coverage online of the announcement of the conclave's election of Jorge Mario Cardinal Bergoglio and his presentation as Pope Francis.

Over the next few days, I read everything I could find about the new pope's previous ministry, and I began to be encouraged that some of the things for which I had personally hoped in a future pope as I prayed for the conclave might come to pass.

Admiration for a Friend of Baptists, and for a Baptist

I was encouraged immediately by the admiration Pope Francis had for Walter Cardinal Kasper, who played a key role in making possible and encouraging the second phase of conversations between the Baptist World Alliance and the Catholic Church from 2006 through 2010. In his first public "Angelus" address in St. Peter's Square on March 17, 2013, Pope Francis said:

> In these days, I have been able to read a book by a cardinal—Cardinal Kasper, a talented theologian, a good theologian—on mercy. And it did me such good, that book, but don't think that I'm publicizing the books of my cardinals. That is not the case! But it did me such good, so much good…Cardinal Kasper said that hearing the word mercy changes everything. It is the best thing that we can hear: it changes the world. A bit of mercy makes the world less cold and more just. We need to understand God's mercy well, this merciful Father who has such patience.[3]

Cardinal Kasper was Secretary of the Pontifical Council for Promoting Christian Unity in the years before and during our conversations. When the Congregation for the Doctrine of the Faith issued the controversial document *Dominus Iesus* in 2000[4] that seemed to say that many non-Catholic churches including Baptist churches should not be regarded as churches, Cardinal Kasper worked behind the scenes to repair the damage. One thing he did toward that end was to encourage the global leadership of the BWA to respond positively to the invitation for dialogue and to promote its desirability within the Vatican.

The appreciation of Francis for this friend of Baptists was an indication of his own ecumenical openness that some of us would later experience firsthand as Baptists, and the decision to highlight Kasper's theology of mercy anticipated a papal ministry that would endeavor to extend the mercy of God to the world. Two years into his papacy, Francis would address a joint session of the U.S. Congress and would mention a Baptist saint, Martin Luther King, Jr., along with Catholics Thomas Merton and Dorothy Day, as American models for seeking the justice God seeks for the world.[5] His commendation of a Baptist as an example of the lived Christian life was remarkable for a pope, but it was also instructive for Baptists, who can recognize non-Baptist Christians as saintly models for our living of the Christian life, too — as indeed many Baptists have already been doing.

I thought that the fact that Pope Francis belonged to the Jesuit order was auspicious for those who hoped for new developments of reform in the life of the Catholic Church, for historically the Jesuits have sometimes been on the outs with the Vatican and have themselves tended to be critical of the Curia. This gave me hope that this would be a pope who would not shrink from seeking to lead the church to be more fully a church of the people and for the people.

Francis, Teacher of the Church

Francis led the church in people-focused directions in significant ways through his role as a teacher of the church. While I will always remember Pope Benedict XVI as the theologian who became Pope, Francis has played an important role in his exercise of the Catholic Church's papal theological teaching authority. Not everything the pope teaches has the degree of authority of an *ex cathedra* definition of Catholic doctrine—the "extraordinary magisterium," never exercised by Benedict or Francis—but papal encyclicals as expressions of the "ordinary magisterium" are important sources of

Catholic theological instruction, and not only for Catholics. I've required my divinity students to read some of the encyclicals of Francis.

In the first year of his papacy, Francis finished an encyclical begun by Benedict: *Lumen Fidei*, "On Faith."[6] While it reflects the interests of his predecessor in the theological sources of authority for the church's faith, Francis emphasized the faith they authorize as what helps the church discern and attend to the sufferings that mark the present order of this world.

Francis' first solo-authored encyclical *Laudato Si'*, "On Care for Our Common Home," may be the most enduringly influential of the trio of encyclicals written in full by Francis.[7] Each year students in my Christian Ethics course read it as one of the texts assigned for our unit on ecological ethics. My first reading of *Laudato Si'* was on the morning of its public release online on June 18, 2015. I was attending the General Assembly of the Cooperative Baptist Fellowship in Dallas, Texas, devoted to the theme "Building Bridges," with bridges crossing racial divides among the principal applications. (Coincidentally but appropriately, the Latin papal title Pontifex means "bridge builder.") We had just learned the previous evening of the murder of nine African American members of Mother Emmanuel A.M.E Church in Charleston, South Carolina, by white supremacist Dylann Roof.

I read quickly through *Laudato Si'* over breakfast with that weighing on my mind, and I was struck by the applicability of its theological framework for ecological justice to the pursuit of racial justice. Its analysis of the human roots of the ecological crisis was nothing less than a theological anthropology—an account of God's intentions for humanity as the image of God. It was an account of God's creation of humanity for relationship: for relationship with God, fellow humanity, and the rest of the created order. The encyclical described how humanity's sinful turn away from the other and toward the self was at the heart of the modern alienated relationship between humanity and creation, identifying the violence that marks human relationships as a chief expression of this alienation. A distorted anthropology accounts for both violence toward creation and violence toward people, and a restorative anthropological vision of the interconnectedness of humanity and of the whole of creation offers the hope of reconciliation and healing both for humanity and for the whole created order to which humanity belongs.

Francis' second encyclical "On Fraternity and Social Friendship" (*Fratelli Tutti*) was issued in October 2020 in the midst of the social isolation experienced during that first year of the COVID-19 pandemic.[8] It made extensive reference to *Laudato Si'* and developed its theological anthropology more fully as a theology of human fraternity that answers to the aversion to the "other" that marks many expressions of contemporary American culture. The other who is other than us is inseparable from our identity as human: to be fully human is to be in relationship with people who aren't like us. When we are in relationship only with those who are like us, we are less than the fullness of the creation of humanity in the image of God.

Francis also in this connection offered the Baptist Martin Luther King, Jr. as an embodied example of a more fully relational theological anthropology with the potential for including diverse others within the bond of human fraternity, formed by the experience of being "othered" by an exclusionary society in the Southern United States. Francis lists King first among the "brothers and sisters who are not Catholics" who particularly inspired him in this connection. Though he doesn't cite it, Francis may have been inspired by King's "Letter from Birmingham Jail." In it, King wrote, "Injustice anywhere is a threat to justice everywhere. We are caught in an inescapable network of mutuality, tied in a single garment of destiny. Whatever affects one directly, affects all indirectly."[9]

Pope Francis issued a third and final encyclical that may have been missed by many Americans preoccupied with their intensifying presidential election cycle, as it was published on October 24, 2024: *Dilexit Nos*, "On the Human and Divine Love of the Heart of Jesus Christ."[10] At the beginning of its concluding section, he wrote:

> 217. The present document can help us see that the teaching of the social Encyclicals *Laudato Si'* and *Fratelli Tutti* is not unrelated to our encounter with the love of Jesus Christ. For it is by drinking of that same love that we become capable of forging bonds of fraternity, of recognizing the dignity of each human being, and of working together to care for our common home.[11]

The remaining three paragraphs of *Dilexit Nos* are worth reading in full, for they summarize well the role of the "People's Pope" as a theological teacher of the church (and not only of Catholic members of the whole church) and what he chose to emphasize in the role:

> 218. In a world where everything is bought and sold, people's sense of their worth appears increasingly to depend on what they can accumulate with the power of money. We are constantly being pushed to keep buying, consuming, and distracting ourselves, held captive to a demeaning system that prevents us from looking beyond our immediate and petty needs. The love of Christ has no place in this perverse mechanism, yet only that love can set us free from a mad pursuit that no longer has room for a gratuitous love. Christ's love can give a heart to our world and revive love wherever we think that the ability to love has been definitively lost.

> 219. The Church also needs that love, lest the love of Christ be replaced with outdated structures and concerns, excessive attachment to our own ideas and opinions, and fanaticism in any number of forms, which end up taking the place of the gratuitous love of God that liberates, enlivens, brings joy to the heart, and builds communities. The wounded side of Christ continues to pour forth that stream which is never exhausted, never passes away, but offers itself time and time again to all those who wish to love as he did. For his love alone can bring about a new humanity.

> 220. I ask our Lord Jesus Christ to grant that his Sacred Heart may continue to pour forth the streams of living water that can heal the hurt we have caused, strengthen our ability to love and serve others, and inspire us to journey together towards a just, solidary, and fraternal world. Until that day when we will rejoice in celebrating together the banquet of the heavenly kingdom in the presence of the risen Lord, who harmonizes all our differences in the light that radiates perpetually from his open heart. May he be blessed forever.[12]

Pope Francis thus concluded his final encyclical with a prayer to Jesus, that he might heal the harm we have caused to the world and help us do the work of reconciliation and justice that God has called us to do.

Baptist Encounters with Francis

I experienced Pope Francis as a person of prayer who humbly invited people to pray for him in December 2018, when our joint commission for the international ecumenical dialogue between the Baptist World Alliance and the Catholic Church met in Rome. We attended the weekly general audience along with about two thousand other people, but afterwards the members of our joint dialogue commission were brought forward and briefly introduced to Pope Francis. He spoke to us in English and said, "Pray for me!" and we assured him that we do. He also said, "If we do not find a way to get together, they will eat us raw!" (which we interpreted as meaning, "they will eat us alive").

In December 2022, our Baptist-Catholic dialogue joint commission again met in Rome, and this time we had a private audience with Pope Francis. At the beginning of the week, we had been told that our private audience with Pope Francis preceding his Wednesday morning general audience would likely be very brief. But after Pope Francis walked into the audience hall and said in Spanish to an Argentinian Catholic theologian on our joint commission whom he recognized, "We did well, didn't we?" (this was the morning following Argentina's World Cup semifinal win over Croatia), he spoke to us at length in Italian, translated into English for us. He shared with us earnestly many things that were on his mind and in his heart, from the war in Ukraine, to ecumenical challenges and opportunities, to how he hoped Baptists could help Catholics fight the "dangers of clericalism," and back to his concerns about Ukraine. He then invited us to join him in praying the Lord's Prayer, each of us in our own language—a profoundly meaningful experience—before greeting each of us individually on his way out of the hall.

That private audience with Pope Francis in December 2022 was memorable for me for another reason that I will always cherish. On behalf of our joint commission, elected BWA President Tomás Mackey, who is also from Argentina, presented Pope Francis with a copy of my book, *Baptists,*

Catholics, and the Whole Church: Partners in the Pilgrimage to Unity, signed by each member of the commission.[13] The book was rooted in the work of the joint commissions for Phase II and Phase III of the Baptist-Catholic dialogue, so we thought it a symbolically appropriate gift.

PRAYING FOR AND WITH POPE FRANCIS

I have prayed for Pope Francis often during his papacy, and I did so with new urgency earlier in February of this year when we learned of his hospitalization and grave condition. In the midst of his illness, he continued to serve God, the church, and the world faithfully. Though diagnosed with acute bronchitis on February 3, on February 10 Francis wrote and published a "Letter of the Holy Father Francis to the Bishops of the United States of America" that denounced the Trump administration's efforts at mass deportation and implicitly but directly rejected the appeal of Catholic Vice President JD Vance to the Augustinian concept of an *ordo amoris*, a "hierarchy" or "ordering" of loves, as a religious justification for directing one's energies and resources to meeting the needs of our own nation rather than caring for migrants and refugees from other nations who come to our nation. He wrote, "The true *ordo amoris* that must be promoted is that which we discover by meditating constantly on the parable of the 'Good Samaritan'… that is, by meditating on the love that builds a fraternity open to all, without exception."[14] Four days later Francis was hospitalized, and I thanked God when he was released from the hospital thirty-eight days later on March 23.

I most recently prayed for Pope Francis on the last weekend of his life when I learned that Vice President Vance was in Rome and seeking to meet with Francis. Vance was granted a very brief meeting with Francis just before Francis appeared in St. Peter's Basilica to deliver his Easter greetings. While I do not know what Francis said to Vance, we do know what Francis said in his final Easter message, which was delivered orally on his behalf by Archbishop Diego Ravelli just after Francis delivered his own brief greetings.[15]

It included what became Francis' final social media post: "Christ is risen! These words capture the whole meaning of our existence, for we were not made for death but for life."[16] Francis also said:

On this day, I would like all of us to hope anew and to revive our trust in others, including those who are different than ourselves, or who come from distant lands, bringing unfamiliar customs, ways of life and ideas! For all of us are children of God!

I appeal to all those in positions of political responsibility in our world not to yield to the logic of fear which only leads to isolation from others, but rather to use the resources available to help the needy, to fight hunger, and to encourage initiatives that promote development. These are the 'weapons' of peace: weapons that build the future, instead of sowing seeds of death! May the principle of humanity never fail to be the hallmark of our daily actions. In the face of the cruelty of conflicts that involve defenseless civilians and attack schools, hospitals, and humanitarian workers, we cannot allow ourselves to forget that it is not targets that are struck, but persons, each possessed of a soul and human dignity.[17]

May we all heed these final preached words of Pope Francis.

Pope Francis has been faithful in fervently praying for God's world, and I am confident that he is continuing to do so. Many of our Catholic brothers and sisters will no doubt ask Francis to pray for them, interceding with God in prayer on their behalf, as they would do during his earthly life. This "intercession of the saints," directly asking departed saints to pray for us, is not a feature of my Baptist tradition. But I do believe that when I am praying, I am praying along with Francis and all other members of the communion of saints who have departed this earthly life and are praying in their life "with the Lord" (2 Cor. 5:8) as they await the resurrection. I am strengthened by the conviction that when I am praying, I am praying along with this particular saint.

I resolved to pray for my Catholic brothers and sisters in their days of mourning the death of Pope Francis, and I began praying for the members of the College of Cardinals who would soon meet in conclave to select the next pope. I shared the worries of many that there might be efforts by some to elect a pope who will turn the Catholic Church in a more rightward direction, away from the openness and concern for social justice that has marked the papacy of Pope Francis. But there were similar worries in

2013—and look what happened! While it had seemed that a traditionalist movement was gaining ground in some quarters of the Catholic Church, I remembered reading that Francis appointed eighty percent of the cardinals who would be eligible to vote in the conclave to choose his successor.

My prayers of thanksgiving for the life of God's faithful servant Pope Francis, prayers for myself that I might heed his summons to be a more faithful follower of Jesus Christ, and prayers for the College of Cardinals to be led by God's Spirit in choosing his successor formed the immediate backdrop for the story told by the remainder of this book.

NOTES

[1] Pope Benedict XVI, "Address of His Holiness Benedict XVI to Members of the Joint International Commission Sponsored by the Baptist World Alliance and the Pontifical Council for Promoting Christian Unity" (December 6, 2007), https://www.vatican.va/content/benedict-xvi/en/speeches/2007/december/documents/hf_ben-xvi_spe_20071206_baptist-alliance.html, accessed 2 July 2025.

[2] Published as Steven R. Harmon, "Free Church Theology, the Pilgrim Church, and the Ecumenical Future," *Journal of Ecumenical Studies* 49, no. 3 (Summer 2014): 420–442.

[3] Pope Francis, "Angelus" (March 17, 2013), https://www.vatican.va/content/francesco/en/angelus/2013/documents/papa-francesco_angelus_20130317.html, accessed 2 July 2025.

[4] Congregation for the Doctrine of the Faith, "Declaration *'Dominus Iesus'* on the Unicity and Salvific Universality of Jesus Christ and the Church" (August 6, 2000), https://www.vatican.va/roman_curia/congregations/cfaith/documents/rc_con_cfaith_doc_20000806_dominus-iesus_en.html, accessed 2 July 2025.

[5] Pope Francis, "Address of the Holy Father," Joint Session of the United States Congress, Washington, D. C. (September 24, 2015), https://www.vatican.va/content/francesco/en/speeches/2015/september/documents/papa-francesco_20150924_usa-us-congress.html, accessed 2 July 2025.

[6] Pope Francis, *Lumen Fidei*, "On Faith" (June 29, 2013), https://www.vatican.va/content/francesco/en/encyclicals/documents/papa-francesco_20130629_enciclica-lumen-fidei.html, accessed 2 July 2025.

[7] Pope Francis, *Laudato Si'*, "On Care for Our Common Home" (May 24, 2015), https://www.vatican.va/content/francesco/en/encyclicals/documents/papa-francesco_20150524_enciclica-laudato-si.html, accessed 2 July 2025.

[8] Pope Francis, *Fratelli Tutti*, "On Fraternity and Social Friendship" (October 3, 2020), https://www.vatican.va/content/francesco/en/encyclicals/documents/papa-francesco_20201003_enciclica-fratelli-tutti.html, accessed 2 July 2025.

[9] Martin Luther King, Jr., "Letter from Birmingham Jail" (April 16, 1963), p. 2, http://okra.stanford.edu/transcription/document_images/undecided/630416-019.pdf, accessed 2 July 2025.

[10] Pope Francis, *Dilexit Nos*, "On the Human and Divine Love of the Heart of Jesus Christ" (October 24, 2024), https://www.vatican.va/content/francesco/en/encyclicals/documents/20241024-enciclica-dilexit-nos.html, accessed 2 July 2025.

[11] Pope Francis, *Dilexit Nos*, 217.

[12] Pope Francis, *Dilexit Nos*, 218–220.

[13] Steven R. Harmon, Baptists, Catholics, and the Whole Church: Partners in the Pilgrimage to Unity (Hyde Park, N.Y.: New City Press, 2021).

[14] Pope Francis, "Letter of the Holy Father Francis to the Bishops of the United States of America," February 10, 2025, https://www.vatican.va/content/francesco/en/letters/2025/documents/20250210-lettera-vescovi-usa.html, accessed 2 July 2025.

[15] Pope Francis, "Homily of His Holiness Pope Francis, Read by Cardinal Angelo Comastri," April 20, 2025, https://www.vatican.va/content/francesco/en/homilies/2025/documents/20250420-omelia-pasqua.html, accessed 2 July 2025.

[16] Pope Francis, "Christ is risen! These words capture the entire meaning of our existence, for we were not made for death but for life," X, 7:15 A.M., April 20, 2025, https://x.com/Pontifex266Arch/status/1913914290685292933, accessed 2 July 2025.

[17] Pope Francis, "Homily" (April 20, 2025).

Chapter 3
Arriving in Rome

In mid-February 2025, when it seemed likely that Pope Francis would not survive his hospitalization in the Gemelli Hospital in Rome, a news editor asked if I would be willing to do advance work on an opinion piece reflecting on the life and legacy of Pope Francis that would be published upon his death. I agreed to do so and began working on it. Francis' condition became more critical in late February, and on March 3 he suffered two episodes of acute respiratory failure. But then his condition stabilized and improved, and he was discharged from the hospital on March 23.

I had already paused my work on the Pope Francis memorial piece a couple of weeks earlier, and I hoped that he might continue to improve. But early on the morning of Monday, April 21, the day after Pope Francis' Easter Sunday public appearance in St. Peter's Square, I reached for my phone to turn off its alarm and saw a notification for a story announcing his death and another notification for a message from a fellow theologian friend sharing the news with me. I rolled out of bed and went straight to the computer to resume work on my article, now with an urgent deadline.

From Home to Rome in Eleven Days

When I submitted the article[1] later that morning, I asked my editor half-jokingly, "Don't suppose you need a correspondent in Rome to cover the conclave?" He replied, "The spirit is willing, but the budget is weak." I told my wife Kheresa about that over dinner that evening and said, "If I were independently wealthy, I'd book a flight to Rome and stay there awhile to observe the election of the new pope and do some writing about it." I could not get that thought out of my brain the rest of the evening. By the next day I had a plan: lacking independent wealth, I needed to pitch my idea to a religious media organization that might be interested in funding what I had in mind. I immediately thought of Good Faith Media, which was formed in 2020 as the merger of *Baptists Today* (originally *SBC Today*, founded in 1983) and the Baptist Center for Ethics (founded in 1991), both of which had been born in the context of the fundamentalist takeover of the Southern Baptist Convention to provide sources of information and perspectives beyond those officially sanctioned by the increasingly ultra-conservative SBC. The work of Good Faith Media and my own work as a professor in Cooperative Baptist Fellowship-affiliated institutions of theological education, founded as alternatives to the official seminaries of the Southern Baptist Convention, have common origins and common cause.

On the evening of Tuesday, April 22, I sent an e-mail message to Mitch Randall, Chief Executive Officer of Good Faith Media, offering to serve as a special correspondent in Rome covering the papal conclave and the beginning of the new pontificate. Mitch had a couple of follow-up questions about my proposal later that evening and early on the morning of Wednesday, April 23. He conferred mid-morning with a couple of his colleagues, who agreed they'd like to move forward with what I proposed, and then called me to discuss details. By that afternoon, I was rescheduling capstone conferences for my students at Gardner-Webb University School of Divinity and making adjustments to final papers and exams so I could wrap up my teaching semester a week early to get to Rome in time for the conclave. On Thursday I applied to the Holy See Press Office for credentials as a temporarily accredited journalist and was interviewed by a reporter for Spectrum News, a North Carolina cable news network, about the death of Pope Francis and his legacy.[2]

After watching coverage of the funeral of Pope Francis on Saturday, April 26 (from a DVR recording, as televised coverage began at 3:30 a.m. Eastern Time), I booked my flights and arranged for lodging in Rome. Traditionally, papal conclaves were expected to begin as early as fifteen days following the death of a pope and no later than 20 days thereafter. That would mean a window for the beginning of the conclave as early as May 6 and as late as May 16. Conclaves from the twentieth century through the present had lasted a minimum of two days and a maximum of four days. So, I booked a flight departing Charlotte for Rome on May 3 and returning on May 14, with a changeable itinerary in the event that the conclave began at the late end of the range of possibilities and/or continued longer than the recent precedents. That afternoon I received a message from a segment producer with the BBC News Washington, D.C. bureau asking if I would be willing to be interviewed live by BBC anchor Carl Nasman at 9:00 p.m. about Pope Francis for a segment broadcast nationally and globally, and after dinner I was in my office on campus wearing a coat and tie, sitting for a live BBC interview.[3] Nasman asked me about what I meant by characterizing Pope Francis as "the People's Pope," my recollections of meeting Pope Francis in connection with our Baptist-Catholic dialogue, my perspective as a Baptist on how Pope Francis viewed and related to other denominations and how he pursued unity with them, and how I interpreted the meaning of Pope Francis' exhortation to "build bridges, not walls" that had been quoted in the funeral Mass homily earlier that day by Cardinal Giovanni Battista Re, dean of the College of Cardinals.[4]

The next morning, not long before the Sunday School hour at St. John's Baptist Church in Charlotte, North Carolina, where I am a member and my wife serves as Minister for Children and Their Families, I received a message from the Holy See Press Office notifying me that I had been granted temporary accredited journalist status and providing instructions for picking up my press credentials upon my arrival in Rome. At the conclusion of the morning worship service, our pastor Dennis Foust invited me to tell the congregation what I'd be doing in Rome beginning the following Sunday.

After the service, church member Kathy Bragg told me that my going to Rome for this occasion reminded her of something in the church's history and the story of her own family. Kathy is the daughter of the late Claude U. Broach, who served as the pastor of St. John's Baptist Church from 1944 until his retirement in 1974, after which he became the first full-time director of the Wake Forest University-Belmont Abbey College Ecumenical Institute. Kathy was remembering how in 1965 her father had travelled to Rome as a Baptist guest for a portion of the Second Vatican Council with the support of his congregation. I was remembering this too as I prepared to travel to Rome myself, as a few years earlier I had researched these events for an invited lecture and subsequent journal article on Broach's pastoral ecumenical activism.[5]

In 1962, preparations for the opening of the Second Vatican Council included invitations to the leaders of Christian world communions to send official ecumenical observers to the Council. In August 1962, the Executive Committee of the Baptist World Alliance declined the invitation. Then in June 1965, the Southern Baptist Convention meeting in Houston, Texas, received from Robert Alley, a professor of religion at the University of Richmond, the following proposed resolution: "I move that this convention appoint a committee composed of the six seminary presidents and direct said committee to select a competent Southern Baptist scholar to attend the fourth session of Vatican Council II as a delegated observer from the Southern Baptist Convention." The proposed resolution was overwhelmingly defeated. Broach was dismayed. Later that summer Broach expressed to his friend Father Cuthbert Allen of Belmont Abbey College his disappointment in the SBC's action. He said, "I hope you know that there are thousands of Baptist ministers and people all over this land who are not in sympathy with this action of the Convention. On the contrary, we are happy over what has happened at Vatican II, and we rejoice in the new spirit and the new relationships which now become possible." Then Broach added ("impulsively," he characterized this next part of the conversation), "You know, I would like to go to Rome on my own, as a Baptist pastor, just to serve as a symbol of the fact that there are multitudes of Baptists who welcome what has happened in Christian history in these tremendous events. Do you suppose there is any way I could go, not as a tourist, but in some accredited fashion, to attend a session in Rome?" Father Allen replied, "It's a great idea! We'll see what can be done."[6] Father Allen went to the Abbot of Belmont Abbey, Father Walter Coggin, who was in Rome as one of the council fathers, who in turn appealed to Monsignor Willibrands of the Secretariat for Promoting Christian Unity, who in turn appointed Broach as an accredited "Visiting Theologian" with access to the proceedings of the Council, free to come to Rome at a time of his choosing and remain at the Council as long as he wanted to do so. Father Allen received this news from Rome and communicated it to Broach on November 1. Broach immediately made plans to go to Rome, with the enthusiastic support of members of St. John's, who provided the funds for the trip.[7] He arrived in Rome in time to observe the final ten days of the Council, November 29 through December 8, 1965, which he chronicled in a series of articles for the *Charlotte Observer* and in an article for *The Baptist Program*, a publication of the SBC Executive Committee.[8] That story features prominently in the collective memory of the congregation regarding their longest-serving pastor and is highlighted in the church's published histories.[9]

On Monday morning, Vatican News announced that in that day's daily meeting of the cardinals present in Rome, they had decided that the conclave would begin on Wednesday, May 7.[10] For me, the next four days were tightly scheduled with teaching final class sessions, holding capstone conferences with graduating students, grading exams and papers and submitting final grades a week early, and attending final school and university faculty meetings of the academic year; I also granted a live radio interview to a station in Raleigh, North Carolina, about the legacy of Pope Francis.[11] On Thursday and Friday, Kheresa and I drove to and from Richmond, Virginia, where she was the keynote preacher for the annual gathering of Virginia Baptist Women in Ministry at the First Baptist Church of Richmond and I took advantage of the opportunity to do recruiting of prospective students for my School of Divinity. Then after lunch on Saturday, Kheresa drove me to Charlotte Douglas International Airport for my flight to Rome.

Arriving in Rome

I arrived in Rome on Sunday morning to a city still mourning the death of Pope Francis. After taking a train from the airport into the city, my taxi from the Rome Termini train station to my lodgings took me past a video billboard spanning half the façade of a downtown building that proclaimed, "ROME EMBRACES POPE FRANCIS WITH LOVE." That weekend, people were continuing daily to stand in line three to four hours to get inside the Basilica of St. Mary Maggiore to stand briefly before the simple tomb of Francis. A few hours before I took a post-dinner stroll to St. Peter's Square to record a brief promo video for my Good Faith Media conclave dispatches, the cardinals currently in Rome—including most of the 133 eligible cardinal electors expected to vote in the conclave—were in St. Peter's Basilica to celebrate the ninth and final memorial Mass of the Novendiali, the nine days of mourning for the death of a pope that began on April 26. And late into Sunday night, St. Peter's Square was filled with at least as many visitors as the throngs who came to behold the Vatican Nativity scene and Christmas tree during the Decembers that our Baptist-Catholic international ecumenical dialogue joint commission had met in Rome.

While continuing to mourn the death of a beloved pope, Rome was also gearing up for the comparatively infrequent occurrence of what is arguably the world's oldest continuously utilized method for selecting the new leader of a large organization. Vatican firefighters had installed on the roof of the Sistine Chapel the temporary chimney from which will issue the color-coded smoke that will communicate to the world the outcome of the voting of the cardinals sealed off from the world: black smoke at the conclusion of a round of voting that fails to achieve the minimum of at least two-thirds of the cardinal electors voting for a single candidate, and white smoke when a round of voting has finally elected a pope.

Hotel vacancies, already a scarce commodity in Rome due to the Jubilee Year proclaimed for 2025 drawing pilgrims to Rome from around the world throughout the year, were now almost nonexistent thanks to the additional influx of thousands of journalists with temporary accreditation from the Holy See Press Office for covering the papal conclave. I was grateful for the hospitality of the Chiesa Evangelica Battista di via del Teatro Valle, a Baptist church in the center of Rome near the Pantheon and the Piazza Navona, which made available to me a guest room in the church only a mile's walk from St. Peter's Basilica. I had previously stayed there for a couple of days in December 2022, when I arrived in Rome in advance of that year's meeting of our Baptist-Catholic ecumenical dialogue to deliver a lecture for the Waldensian Faculty of Theology in Rome where many Baptist candidates for the ministry receive their theological education and another lecture for the local Baptist association of churches. When I arrived at the church not long after noon, pastor Simone Caccamo took me straight to the after-worship church meal in time for the soup course and subsequent courses. I enjoyed a delightful lunch conversation with a Lutheran doctoral student in theology from Finland who was doing dissertation research in Rome, along with his friend from Finland who had come to visit him in Rome after a few days of rock climbing in the Italian Alps.

Before dinner on Sunday, I walked by the Domus Internationalis Paulus VI, a guest house for Catholic clergy visiting Rome where Cardinal Jorge Mario Bergoglio had stayed ahead of the 2013 conclave and to which he famously returned after the conclave as Pope Francis to pay his hotel bill. I had stayed there when our Baptist-Catholic dialogue had met in Rome in 2007, 2009, 2018, and 2022, but that afternoon I was interested in seeing whether there were any signs of cardinals staying in Rome ahead of the conclave coming and going. There weren't any clerical comings or goings during my brief period of observation, but this was likely because the cardinals would have been wrapping up their final memorial Mass at St. Peter's Basilica around that time.

In addition to the daily memorial Masses of the Novendiali, the cardinals present in Rome had been assembling in daily congregations to hear from one another about their sense of the current state of the Catholic Church and concerns about its future. These congregations were continuing beyond the Novendiali until the day before the start of the conclave begins; the next morning, I would begin receiving twice-daily briefings on the conclave along with the press pool from Matteo Bruni, director of the Holy See Press Office, regarding the substance of the cardinals' discussions.

Once the conclave began on Wednesday, how long would it last? Modern conclaves (from the twentieth century through the present) had been concluded within four days, and the past two conclaves extended only two days. Some analysts suggested that this one might last longer for two reasons. First, there was a larger number of cardinal electors than in previous conclaves—135 instead of 120, though there were expected to be only 133 in light of announcements by two cardinal electors that they would be unable to travel to Rome for health reasons. Second, the intentionality of Pope Francis in diversifying the College of Cardinals globally meant that many cardinals did not know each other. However, some observers of the Catholic Church pointed out that the opposite might be true: the three-year Synod on Synodality convened by Pope Francis in 2021 had occasioned many additional opportunities for the cardinals to come together, observe one another in action, and get to know each other informally. This familiarity could make the movement toward the election of a candidate by the requisite two-thirds majority a swifter process than might have been the case apart from this synodal process. The next chapter of this book will explain the significance of the Synod on Synodality for the 2025 conclave to elect the successor to Pope Francis.

NOTES

[1] Steven R. Harmon, "Remembering the 'People's Pope'," *Baptist News Global* (April 21, 2025), https://baptistnews.com/article/remembering-the-peoples-pope/, accessed 2 July 2025.

[2] Jennifer Roberts, "'Unity': Gardner-Webb professor spotlights late pope's legacy of overcoming divisions among Christians," Spectrum News 1, Charlotte, NC, April 25, 2025, https://spectrumlocalnews.com/nc/charlotte/news/2025/04/24/professor-spotlighting-pope-s-efforts-to-overcome-divisions-in-christian-communities-, accessed 19 June 2025.

[3] Carl Nasman, interview of Steven Harmon, BBC News, April 26, 2025, https://youtu.be/jaPWLnScxKg, accessed 2 July 2025.

[4] Cardinal Giovanni Battista Re, "Homily of His Eminence Cardinal Giovanni Battista Re, Dean of the College of Cardinals," St. Peter's Square, April 26, 2025, https://www.vatican.va/content/vatican/en/special/sede-vacante/sede-vacante-2025/20250426-messa-esequiale-francesco.html, accessed 2 July 2025.

[5] Steven R. Harmon, "Claude Broach, Pastoral Ecumenical Activist: How a Southern Baptist Pastor Got Invited to Vatican II, Was Eulogized by an Abbott, and Influenced the Quest for Christian Unity," delivered as the annual Carlyle Marney Lecture at Carson-Newman University, Jefferson City, Tennessee, October 31, 2019; idem, "A Word About…Claude Broach, Pastoral Ecumenical Activist," *Review and Expositor* 118, no. 1 (February 2021): 11–17.

[6] Claude U. Broach, *Before It Slips My Mind* (Charlotte, NC: Delmar Printing Co., 1974), 88.

[7] Ibid., 88–90.

[8] Claude U. Broach, "A Baptist Pastor at Vatican II," *The Baptist Program* (April 1966): 20.

[9] Richard L. Young and J. Kenneth Sanford, *Fifty Favored Years: A History of St. John's Baptist Church* (Charlotte, NC: St. John's Baptist Church, 1972), 20–21; J. Kenneth Sanford, *St. John's Baptist Church: The First 90 Years* (Charlotte, NC: St. John's Baptist Church, 2012), 10; Sally Young, "Our Story," in *Faithfully Active, Actively Faithful: A 100 Year History of St. John's Baptist Church*, ed. Fredda Fender Kimball (Charlotte, NC: St. John's Baptist Church, 2024), 35.

[10] Lisa Zengarini and Devin Watkins, "Conclave to elect new Pope to begin on May 7th," *Vatican News* (April 28, 2025), https://www.vaticannews.va/en/vatican-city/news/2025-04/conclave-elect-new-pope-cardinals-beginning-date-may-2025.html, accessed Jun 19, 2025.

[11] Jeff Hamlin, "Steven Harmon: NC Professor on the Late Pope Francis," WPTF Afternoon News, Raleigh, NC, April 28, 2025, https://rss.com/podcasts/wptf-afternoon-news/2005540/, accessed 19 June 2025.

Chapter 4
Anticipating the Conclave

Monday, May 5, was my first full day in Rome covering preparations for the papal conclave that would convene on Wednesday afternoon. It began with the requisite caffeinated fuel for the day from the best coffee place in Rome, according to Catholic theologian Peter Casarella, who introduced it to me during the first Rome meeting of Phase II of our Baptist-Catholic ecumenical dialogue in 2007: Sant' Eustachio Il Caffè at 82 Piazza Sant' Eustachio, which in the providence of God was a mere 250 feet from my lodgings at the beginning of my walk to Vatican City. Enjoying a cappuccino doppio accompanied by a caffè doppio (a double cappuccino and a double espresso) en route to the Holy See Press Office would become a daily ritual. (I told my wife Kheresa, who gave me good-natured grief via text message about what I was enjoying, that I ordered the second beverage for her vicarious enjoyment.)

After picking up my press credentials from the Holy See Press Office at Via della Conciliazione 54 (on the right side of the street leading into St. Peter's Square), I settled into the daily routine of journalists covering the lead-up to the conclave: morning writing using the Vatican briefing room as a work space, a 1:00 p.m. press briefing from Holy See Press Office Director Matteo Bruni, afternoon writing in the briefing room, and an 8:00 PM press briefing from Bruni, followed by consolidating notes from the briefings and responses to questions from the press pool in preparation for writing the next dispatch. All this was of course interspersed with the enjoyment of nourishment from nearby eateries. (I discovered that in Rome, one can almost select a restaurant at random and be assured of a fine culinary experience. The menus are comparable, and the food is invariably delicious.)

In the briefing room, I recognized Colleen Dulle, Associate Editor at *America* magazine and co-host of America Media's "Inside the Vatican" podcast. I introduced myself to her and let her know of my appreciation for her podcast, to which I'd been listening every time an episode dropped from the death of Pope Francis through my time in Rome. It was an indispensable resource for orienting me to the events I was now covering. When I was back in my guest room Monday night, I watched a video clip from the recording of a new episode of "Inside the Vatican" that morning and realized that when I met Colleen, I also met Scott Detrow, weekend host of NPR's "All Things Considered" program who had hosted the show from Rome that weekend and was there to cover the conclave for NPR. Scott was a guest for the "Inside the Vatican" podcast to talk about what it was like for secular media to cover the conclave. The name didn't register initially when we were introduced, but his voice sounded familiar, and now I knew why. A month after returning home from the conclave, I learned that Scott and NPR senior editor of religion and spirituality Daniel Burke were co-authoring a forthcoming biography of the new pope.[1]

While waiting for my first briefing as part of the press pool, I remembered having a similar experience much earlier in life. As a high school student, I had served on the school newspaper staff, ultimately as editor, and had a part-time job as a sports correspondent reporting on my school's home varsity football games for *The Cameron Herald*, a newspaper serving a town about fifteen miles from my hometown of Rosebud. I competed in interscholastic journalism competitions, and in my senior year I advanced to the state feature writing competition at the University of Texas in Austin. Before writing our stories, we participated in a press conference with a mystery interviewee about whom we would write, who turned out to be Kathy Cronkite, daughter of CBS Evening News anchor Walter Cronkite, who was working at an Austin radio station and five years earlier had published a book on the experiences of children of celebrities.[2] During the next week in Rome, I would realize that the vocational skills required for research and writing in historical theology and for journalism were not dissimilar: both required rigorous investigation of something before writing about it, and in the case of journalism, the subject of investigation and writing is something currently happening that must be contextualized by investigating the history that leads to it.

The Cardinals Prepare for the Conclave: Daily Congregations

Monday's press briefings focused on the activities of the cardinals, who had been meeting in daily congregations each day since the funeral of Pope Francis. For the first time in this period, on Monday there were two congregations held instead of a single congregation meeting, both a morning session and an afternoon session, in order to make time for all the cardinals who had indicated that they wished to speak. Between the two sessions that day, a total of forty-six cardinals made contributions.

As of Monday, all 133 of the cardinals who would participate in the conclave as "cardinal electors" were present in Rome. All cardinals present in Rome were eligible to meet in the daily congregations, including those who are 80 years old and above and therefore were not eligible to vote in the conclave. These non-voting cardinals can have an influence on a conclave through their brief speeches in the congregations, called "interventions" in the English usage of the Vatican, which they offer along with those cardinal electors who wish to speak. In the morning congregation there were 179 cardinals present, of whom 132 were electors, and in the afternoon congregation there were 170 cardinals total and again 132 electors.

In the 2025 conclave, there were 135 members of the College of Cardinals who were under 80 years old and eligible to vote in the conclave. Two cardinals, one from Kenya and one from Spain, had given notice that they would be unable to travel to Rome for the conclave due to health reasons, bringing the number of electors down to 133. There is no provision for remote voting; cardinals must be present in the conclave in order to cast ballots.

The notation that there were 132 electors present in both morning and evening congregations raised the question: is the missing elector ill? Vatican press director Bruni had no information to provide regarding that elector's condition, but he did note that there is a provision for what would happen if a cardinal becomes ill during the conclave and cannot be present in the Sistine Chapel to cast his ballot but is confined to his room in the attached residence for cardinals sequestered in the conclave, the "House of Saint Martha" (Domus Sanctae Marthae in Latin and Casa Santa Marta in Italian; it is often referred to simply as Santa Marta). In such a case, a delegation of three randomly chosen cardinals would go to the ill elector's room, collect the ballot, and take it to be cast in the Sistine Chapel along with the other ballots. This would not be considered remote voting, since the ill elector is nonetheless physically present at the conclave and shares with the other electors the experience of being separated from all communications with the outside world that might influence their votes. When the cardinals enter the conclave, they surrender all electronic devices—mobile phones, computers, etc.—to be placed in a sealed plastic bag and returned to them only after the conclusion of the conclave.

The interventions (speeches) made by cardinals in the daily congregations prepare the way for the conclave by making one another aware of the experiences of the church in the regions where they live, their sense of the challenges faced by the church locally and globally, and their perspectives regarding the sort of leader the church needs in a new pope.

They can also provide previews of potential candidates for the papacy. It had been reported that in the 2013 conclave that elected Jorge Mario Bergoglio as Pope Francis, the brief intervention by Bergoglio played a role in his eventual election on the fifth ballot of that conclave. Cardinals recognized to speak were granted seven minutes but routinely exceeded that limit. Bergoglio finished his speech in less than five minutes, and some of his fellow cardinals were said to comment to each other on how compellingly and succinctly he stated the issues confronting the church. Gerard O'Connell, associate editor and Vatican correspondent for *America*, a monthly magazine published by members of the Jesuit order in the United States, wrote this about Bergoglio's March 9 intervention in his book, *The Election of Pope Francis: An Inside Account of the Conclave That Changed History*, which is widely regarded as the definitive account of the 2013 conclave:

> The archbishop of Buenos Aires, Jorge Mario Bergoglio, was one of the seventeen [who spoke in that daily congregation]. He delivered

an unforgettable three-and-a-half-minute intervention in Spanish that catapulted him onto the radar screen of many electors. That speech is now considered as one of the decisive moments in the lead-in to the conclave, a turning point. He touched hearts, and many more cardinals began to see him as the candidate to succeed Benedict. Cardinal [Seán Patrick] O'Malley [the Archbishop of Boston from 2003 to 2024], who was sitting behind him in the synod hall, recalled that moment much later. "Everybody had spoken about everything, and again about everything. But Bergoglio said something new and fresh. Cardinals took note."[3]

After providing the full text of Bergoglio's intervention (to which O'Connell had access because Cardinal Jaime Lucas Ortega y Alamino, the Archbishop of Havana, Cuba, had requested it from Bergoglio that day, read it at Mass in Havana following the conclave, and then published it in the diocesan newspaper), O'Connell noted this about the cardinals' reaction:

> Cardinals applauded when Bergoglio finished speaking. In his autobiography, *An English Spring*, Cardinal [Cormac] Murphy-O'Connor [Archbishop of Westminster, United Kingdom from 2000 to 2009] reported what happened next: "There was stillness when he sat down. I looked at the faces of the cardinals around me. Many were moved by what he said. This was the moment, I think, when some of them began to wonder if they might not have heard the voice of the man who would lead the church to recover its vigor and give it a fresh sense of direction."[4]

Might one of the cardinals in the preparations for this conclave offer a similarly significant intervention, I wondered?

In Monday's congregation sessions, cardinals spoke of qualities that the future pope should possess. As Bruni summarized this aspect of the cardinals' speeches, the pope must be "a figure who must be present, close, capable of being a bridge and a guide…favoring access to communion for a disoriented humanity marked by the crisis of the world order; a shepherd close to the real life of the people." Bruni said that the cardinals also emphasized that the pope is called to be a "true pastor" who is able to "go beyond the confines of the Catholic Church" to promote dialogue and build relationships with people who belong to other religious traditions and cultures.

Several cardinals who spoke on Monday mentioned the mission of the church in relation to challenges that the church must address. The church must embrace "*caritas*" (love/charity) as central in fulfilling its calling to provide relief, defend the poor, and bear witness to the justice of the Gospel. They characterized the church as a missionary church that, in the words of Bruni's summary, "must not withdraw into herself, but rather accompany every man and woman towards the living experience of the mystery of God."

Challenges this missionary church must address mentioned by the cardinals include care for creation, war, and migration. Several cardinals offered testimonies about the effects of the violent conflicts taking place in their countries. After Bruni's summary, a journalist asked if the war in Ukraine was mentioned specifically, and Bruni replied that cardinals from Africa and Asia had spoken of wars in those regions. The cardinals identified migration as a significant issue, speaking of migrants as "a gift for the church" and of the urgency of the church's task of accompanying migrants and supporting their faith during their journeys and in the countries where they arrive.

One cardinal in the morning congregation session noted the presence of such a large number of journalists in Rome to cover the conclave as a sign that the Gospel the church proclaims remains relevant for today's world and as a reminder of the responsibility that the church has to the world.

During the opportunity for questions in one of Monday's press briefings, a journalist asked whether the cardinals had spoken of women in the church. Bruni responded that there was discussion of the role of laypeople in the church, without specific reference to their gender, so there was not at this point a discussion of the role of women except in general terms of the participation of laypeople in the "synodality" of the church.

Synodality and the Conclave

This mention of synodality in the press briefing brings up a key aspect of the context of this particular papal conclave in the life of the Catholic Church. The term comes from the Greek word *synodos*, which connotes something like "being together on the way." Pope Francis announced in 2020 that the following year he would convene a synod devoted to helping the Catholic

Church become more fully communal in its deliberations, with input not only from the clergy but from the laity, and not only from Catholics but from other Christian traditions, other religions, and non-religious persons.

The "synodal path" of the Synod on Synodality involved three phases: a local diocesan phase in 2020 and 2021, a continental regional phase in 2022 and 2023, and a universal phase convened at the Vatican in 2023 and 2024. The emphasis in each phase was on listening to voices at each level and synthesizing those discussions so that they could be taken into account in the next phase. During the local diocesan phase, a Catholic parish held one of these listening sessions at Gardner-Webb University so that local college students, and not only Catholic students among them, might be able to speak of their own experiences and voice their own questions. Baptist World Alliance General Secretary Elijah Brown participated in the opening prayer vigil of the universal phase of the synod in St. Peter's Square on September 30, 2023,[5] and Baptist theologians Elizabeth Newman (USA) and Valérie Duval-Poujol served as Baptist "fraternal delegates" to meetings of the Synod in Rome that followed.[6] I later contributed the chapter on "Baptists and Synodality" to a book that grew out of a series of conferences supporting the work of the Synod on Synodality by exploring how synodality functions in various non-Catholic Christian traditions.[7] I argued that while Baptists may not employ the term to describe it, they do practice a form of congregationally-located synodality through their practices of congregational discernment that, ideally, listen for the voice of God not only in the voices of the members of the congregation but also in voices from well beyond the local congregation that are brought to bear on their discernment of how they might become a faithful community of followers of Jesus Christ in their particular time and place.

One question that loomed over the 2025 papal conclave was this: will the successor to Pope Francis continue and implement this emphasis on the Catholic Church as a communion of discernment that listens to all voices, or will he offer qualifications or encourage redirections of the synodal path?

Predictions for the Conclave?

Between Monday's press briefings, I saw *America* magazine editor at large and frequent ABC News commentator on Catholicism Fr. James Martin,

S.J. (the initials following his name indicate that like Pope Francis, he belongs to the Jesuit order) at a restaurant on Borgo Santo Spirito next to the headquarters of the Jesuit order, Il Wine Bar De' Penitenzieri, which quickly became my favorite Vatican City restaurant. I introduced myself to him as a Baptist theologian from North Carolina covering the conclave for Good Faith Media. He observed, "It must be interesting for a Southern Baptist to cover the conclave," and I was able to tell him about the "Baptists Formerly Known as Southern," a.k.a. the Cooperative Baptist Fellowship that became my ecclesial home in the wake of the rightward turn of the Southern Baptist Convention.

I asked Fr. Martin if he had any predictions for the length of the conclave, and he said, "I think it will be a short one." He speculated that in the present context, the cardinals would not want a lengthier conclave to give the impression that they are divided among themselves.

We would soon see whether Fr. Martin was right about this. Modern conclaves since the beginning of the twentieth century have been concluded within four days. The shortest was in 1939, when Pope Pius XII was elected early on the second day of the conclave on the third ballot. In 1978, Pope John Paul II was elected on the eighth ballot, which took place on the third day of the conclave. Pope Benedict XVI was elected on the fourth ballot on the second day of the 2005 conclave, and Pope Francis was likewise elected on the second day of the 2013 conclave, but on the fifth ballot.

On Wednesday afternoon, the cardinals will have one round of voting after the 4:00 p.m. opening Mass and then retire for the evening, on the assumption that they will not reach the required two-thirds majority in the first round. On Thursday and each subsequent day, there will be four rounds of voting, two in the morning and two in the afternoon/early evening, until the two-thirds majority is reached.

Notes

[1] Scott Detrow (@scottdetrow_npr), "Big news! NPR Senior Religion & Spirituality editor Daniel Burke and I are teaming up to write a biography of Pope Leo!", Threads, June 25, 2025, https://www.threads.com/@scottdetrow_npr/post/DLU7jbJMZad?xmt=AQF0d5ZZf0un7ETHGr DaU3KHJjmKCYUyxZ-GxxKSBBfsUw, accessed 27 June 2025.

[2] Kathy Cronkite, *On the Edge of the Spotlight: Celebrities' Children Speak Out About Their Lives* (New York: Morrow, 1981).

³ Gerard O'Connell, *The Election of Pope Francis: An Inside Account of the Conclave That Changed History* (Maryknoll, NY: Orbis Books, 2019), 153.

⁴ Ibid., 154–155. Though he does not provide bibliographical details in his book's endnotes, O'Connell's quotation of Cardinal Murphy-O'Connor's book is from Cormac Murphy-O'Connor, *An English Spring: Memoirs* (London: Bloomsbury, 2015).

⁵ Ken Camp, "BWA leader joins ecumenical prayer vigil in Rome," *Baptist Standard* (October 2, 2023), https://baptiststandard.com/news/world/bwa-leader-joins-ecumenical-prayer-vigil-in-rome/, accessed June 20, 2025.

⁶ Jeff Brumley, "She was the only Baptist and only woman fraternal delegate at a Vatican synod," *Baptist News Global* (November 28, 2023), https://baptistnews.com/article/she-was-the-only-baptist-and-the-only-woman-at-a-vatican-synod/, accessed June 20, 2025; Ken Camp, "Baptist praises process followed in Catholic Synod," *Baptist Standard* (November 3, 2023), https://baptiststandard.com/news/faith-culture/baptist-praises-process-followed-in-catholic-synod/, accessed June 20, 2025.

⁷ Steven R. Harmon, "Baptists and Synodality," chapter in *Listening to the West: Synodality in Western Ecclesial Traditions*, ed. Institute for Ecumenical Studies of the Angelicum (Collana Ut Unum Sint, no. 5; Vatican City: Libreria Editrice Vaticana, 2024), 273–282.

Chapter 5
Who Might Become Pope?

The cardinals wrapped up their preparations for the conclave on Tuesday, May 6. They met that morning for a final pre-conclave congregation, after which Holy See Press Office director Matteo Bruni delivered this summary to the press corps in the briefing room:

> The twelfth and final Congregation of Cardinals opened this morning at 9.00, as usual, with a moment of prayer.
> There were 173 Cardinals present, of whom 130 were Electors. There were 26 contributions, dealing with multiple topics.
> Among the main themes that emerged was the reaffirmation that many of the reforms promoted by Pope Francis need to be continued: the fight against abuse, economic transparency, reorganization of the Curia, synodality, commitment to peace and care for creation. The responsibility of the Church in these areas is deeply felt and shared.
> A central theme of the reflection was that of communion, indicated as an essential vocation for the new Pontiff. The profile of a shepherd Pope, a teacher of humanity, capable of embodying the face of a Samaritan Church, close to the needs and wounds of humanity, was outlined. In times marked by wars, violence and strong polarization, a strong need is felt for a spiritual guide who offers mercy, synodality and hope.
> Some contributions also dealt with questions of a canonical nature, reflecting on the power of the Pope.

The theme of divisions within the Church and in society, and the way in which the Cardinals are called to exercise their role in relation to the Papacy, was addressed.

Mention was made of the World Day of the Poor, to be held on the Sunday before the solemnity of Christ the King; it was emphasized that these two events can be interpreted in relation to each other, recognizing the living presence of Christ in the poor and recalling that the true kingship of the Gospel is manifested in service.

The Cardinals spoke about the need to make the meetings of the College of Cardinals more significant on the occasion of Consistories, and to promote Christian initiation and ongoing formation as authentic missionary acts.

The martyrs of the faith were recalled, especially in those lands where Christians suffer persecution or are deprived of religious freedom. Among the pastoral emergencies, the commitment to decisively tackle climate change, recognized as a global and ecclesial challenge, was also reiterated.

The Cardinals reflected again on the date for the celebration of Easter, the Council of Nicaea and ecumenical dialogue.

The Congregation concluded with the reading of an official declaration: an appeal addressed to the parties involved in various international conflicts. The Cardinals invoked a permanent ceasefire and the start of negotiations leading to a just and lasting peace, with respect for human dignity and the common good.

During this morning's meeting, the annulment of the Fisherman's Ring and the lead seal was carried out.

Finally, some practical arrangements were made regarding the programme for the Cardinal Electors during the Conclave.

The meeting ended at 12.30. No further General Congregations are scheduled.[1]

On Tuesday afternoon, the cardinals moved into their secure and sequestered residence for the conclave at Casa Santa Marta, and I turned my attention to reflecting on the reading I'd done over the past several days of a great quantity of published speculation about whom the cardinals might elect as the new pope. Two months before the start of the conclave, Spanish Vatican journalist Javier Martínez-Brocal, who covered the 2005 conclave that elected Benedict XVI and the 2013 conclave that elected Francis, observed that the question one should be asking is not "Who will be the next pope?" but rather "What kind of pope are the cardinals looking for?"[2] In the cardinals' pre-conclave daily congregations from the day following the death of Pope Francis through Tuesday morning, they had made clear the kind of pope they hoped to elect: not necessarily Pope Francis II, but definitely someone who would continue to serve the church and the world in ways comparable to Francis and who would carry forward some of his key emphases: "a shepherd Pope, a teacher of humanity, capable of embodying the face of a Samaritan Church, close to the needs and wounds of humanity," who "[i]n times marked by wars, violence and strong polarization" would be "a spiritual guide who offers mercy, synodality and hope."[3]

Who might become pope in this conclave? In the days before the conclave, I had read multiple articles quoting John L. Allen Jr.'s observation that began his *National Catholic Reporter* list of twenty possible candidates for succeeding Pope John Paul II in the conclave of 2005: "the trash heaps of church history are littered with the carcasses of journalists who have tried to predict the next pope."[4] While I was not keen on volunteering my own carcass by making short lists or predictions, I did have some pre-conclave thoughts about how we might think about the *papabili* (an Italian term popularly applied to cardinals thought to be viable candidates to become pope) as well as about whom the eventual new pope might be.

POPES AND CATEGORIES

It is hard for many of us to resist the temptation to map possible successors to Pope Francis onto the polarizations of American Christianity and its civil context. We may regard them as conservative or liberal, traditionalist or progressive. In terms of those categories, many might consider Benedict XVI to have been a conservative/traditionalist pope and Francis to have been a liberal/progressive pope. Thus, the question many American Christians may have going into the conclave might be framed: will the new pope be more conservative like Benedict or more liberal like Francis?

I suggest that a more helpful set of categories for thinking about potential popes and where they might be positioned on a theological spectrum is rooted in two emphases that marked the work of the Second Vatican Council (1962–1965).

It's commonplace to think of Vatican II as a liberalizing council in comparison with the First Vatican Council (1869–1870), which is typically understood as a more conservative articulation of Catholic faith and practice. There's truth in this comparison. Vatican I in many ways was a conservative reaction against developments of Western modernity in the late nineteenth century, analogous to the way the conservative North American Protestantism that would become evangelicalism reacted against the same developments in that era. Papal infallibility was one of the conservative Catholic reactions, and biblical infallibility was one of the conservative Protestant reactions.

Vatican II, then, did represent a more positive constructive engagement with the modern world, in contrast to Vatican I's conservative reaction against it. But this difference from the dynamics of Vatican I was the result of two interrelated emphases that yielded something different from the earlier council.

One emphasis of Vatican II has been described with the Italian word *aggiornamento*, which means something like "updating." Vatican II represents an updating of the Catholic tradition in bringing it more fully into constructive dialogue with the modern world. This is the major reason Vatican II has been regarded as a liberalizing council.

But *aggiornamento*, updating, was not the only thing that Vatican II sought to accomplish. *Aggiornamento* went hand-in-hand with an emphasis that has been described with the French word *ressourcement* (two s's), which looks like it might mean "resourcing" (one s) but suggests something like a return to or retrieval of earlier sources of the Christian tradition (re-sourcing) that may have been neglected or forgotten but that are needed by the church for constructive engagement with the contemporary world. A French term is employed in this case because it was early-to-mid-twentieth-century French Catholic theologians such as Jean Danielou, Yves Congar, and Henri de Lubac who shaped this aspect of the work of Vatican II. *Ressourcement* does retrieve resources from earlier expressions of the Christian tradition, which may seem like a conservative endeavor. But it does so critically, which is not what a reactionary traditionalism does.[5]

It can be argued that each pope from the beginning of the Second Vatican Council onward has been in continuity with both of the interrelated emphases of that council: the progressive engagement of the world represented by *aggiornamento*, as well as the critical recovery of the riches of the Christian tradition so that their relevance for the mission of the church in the modern world may be recovered (and in some sense conserved) represented by *ressourcement*.

Each of the popes of Vatican II and beyond embodied both *ressourcement* and *aggiornamento* in their exercise of the papal office, but with varying weight behind each of the interrelated emphases. Most recently, Pope Benedict XVI, who was a "peritus" (theological advisor) at the Second Vatican Council in his earlier work as an academic theologian, leaned heavily into the *ressourcement* dimension of the legacy of that council, and Pope Francis embodied especially its *aggiornamento* trajectory. But for both, the two emphases remained intertwined, so that neither can be neatly categorized as conservative or liberal.

In this connection, it's interesting to read John L. Allen Jr.'s paragraph on then-Cardinal Jorge Mario Bergoglio in his overview of twenty *papabili* ahead of the 2005 conclave that elected instead Pope Benedict:

> Bergoglio, a Jesuit, was a trained chemist before deciding to become a priest. He is seen as an accomplished intellectual, having studied theology in Germany. His leading role during the Argentinean economic crisis in 2002 has burnished his reputation as a voice of conscience and has also made him a potent symbol of the costs globalization can impose on the Third World. Within the Jesuits, Bergoglio's reputation is mixed. He was appointed provincial in Buenos Aires in 1973, and at a time when many Latin American Jesuits were moving into the social apostolate, he insisted on a more traditional, spiritual approach. Bergoglio is today close to the Comunione e Liberazione movement. He comes across as traditional theologically, but open and compassionate.[6]

(It's also worth noting in this connection that Allen had written in another National Catholic Reporter article prior to the 2005 conclave, "In analyzing the selection of John Paul's successor…there are only a handful of things that can be said with certainty," among which he included, "it is overwhelmingly likely that the next pope will not be American"[7]—a truism repeated frequently before the conclaves in 2013 and 2025.) Bergoglio's theologically traditional reputation contributed to his perception as a candidate acceptable to more conservative cardinals in the 2013 conclave, but as Pope Francis he became known for being "open and compassionate." In many ways he conserved traditional theological commitments, yet he applied them in ways that pushed in new directions of openness that surprised some of the cardinals who elected him.

Will the majority of the cardinal electors seek someone who will continue Pope Francis' warm, open engagement? Will they prefer a pope who may offer doctrinal and moral clarity where some of them may have perceived Francis as too ambiguous? Or in light of today's violent conflicts in many places in the world and a growing attraction to populist authoritarian movements, might they opt for someone with qualities and skills that lend themselves to diplomacy? While I myself did not come up with a short list of *papabili*, I did take note of three possibilities identified by many journalists.

Possible *Papabili*

Ahead of the conclave, Vatican Secretary of State Cardinal Pietro Parolin received much press as a front runner.[8] He was appointed to this role by Pope Francis and has extensive diplomatic experience that might be appealing to electors in light of current global circumstances. But according to an oft-repeated adage about conclaves, "he who goes in as pope comes out a cardinal."

Some observers of the pre-conclave congregations of the cardinals believed that Parolin's place at the top of lists of *papabile* might already have been torpedoed by a speech made by Cardinal Beniamino Stella, perceived by many as a campaigner behind the scenes for Parolin's candidacy. (Stella, 83, was not eligible to vote in the conclave.) During a daily congregation on April 30, Stella explicitly attacked Francis for having bypassed the tradition of the church linking governance to ordination by opening positions of governance in the Vatican to laypersons, including lay women. It was reported that many cardinals were shocked by this break with Francis by someone linked closely with Parolin.[9]

It had been suggested that Cardinal Matteo Maria Zuppi, the Archbishop of Bologna, was an alternative to Parolin who has extensive diplomatic experience and would represent continuity with the papacy of Francis.[10] He worked closely with the Community of Sant'Egidio, a lay-led community that engages in ecumenical work with the poor and migrants and is involved extensively in peacemaking initiatives. Zuppi was instrumental in negotiating peace agreements in conflicts in Africa.

Another perceived as representing continuity with Francis was Cardinal Luis Antonio Gokim Tagle of the Philippines, to the point that he had been nicknamed "the Asian Francis."[11] During the period of the pre-conclave congregation meetings, German Cardinal Walter Kasper, who at 92 could not take part in the vote, told the Italian newspaper *La Stampa* he was sure the electors would choose someone who would continue the agenda of Pope Francis.[12]

There were several other names repeated in journalists' lists of *papabili*. One that appears only in a few such lists was South Korean Cardinal Lazzaro You Heung-sik.[13] I mention him here because I was personally intrigued as the father of a Korean son by the possibility that Heung-sik could become pope. But I was also encouraged by reading that he has been actively involved in the Focolare movement, a lay-led Catholic ecumenical movement founded by Catholic laywoman Chiara Lubich that constitutionally requires its president to be a laywoman. Among its ventures is New City Press, the publisher of my book *Baptists, Catholics, and the Whole Church: Partners in the Pilgrimage to Unity*.[14]

A Catholic friend in California with whom I corresponded while in Rome suggested to me that a pope from Asia might resist the polarizations of the Western church in ways that would be beneficial for the whole church that includes the Western church. He noted that Asian Catholicism in some ways has more deeply received Vatican II in a manner that transcends divided Western responses to it.

Cardinal Kasper, who retired a few years ago as Secretary of what is now the Dicastery for Promoting Christian Unity, was instrumental in making possible Phase II of the Baptist-Catholic ecumenical dialogue that met 2006–2010, and during our 2009 meeting in Rome he joined our joint commission for a memorable session in which he informally shared his candid perspectives on ecumenism. His confidence shared in an interview with an Italian journalist that the cardinals would elect someone who would carry forward the legacy of Pope Francis was mentioned above. This is what he said:

> I believe that there is a very clear expectation [that] people want a pope to follow Francis—a pastor who knows the language of the heart, who does not close himself in palaces … of course, there are also cardinals who hope for a change of direction with respect to Francis. But my impression … is that the majority of cardinals are in favor of continuity [with Francis].[15]

As a non-Catholic observer of Catholicism who believes that the selection of the next pope has significant implications for all Christians and the whole world, I hoped that Kasper would prove to be right.

But I also thought that it would be helpful for us to resist categorizing whomever would be elected pope as a liberal or a conservative, as a progressive or a traditionalist. The next pope would surely embody the interrelationship of *ressourcement* (retrieval of the tradition for the needs of the present) and *aggiornamento* (updating the church's engagement with the world) in ways that may be more like Francis or more like Benedict. But like Francis in particular, he is likely to surprise us with the manner in which his papacy relates the two emphases to one another.

NOTES

[1] Holy See Press Office, "Information for Journalists," May 6, 2025, https://press.vatican.va/content/salastampa/en/comunicazioni/2025/05/06/250506a.html, accessed 23 June 2025.

[2] Sacha Biazzo, "*I Vaticanisti*: Meet the Reporters Covering Pope Francis," Columbia Journalism Review (February 28, 2025), https://www.cjr.org/world/vatican-reporters-pope-francis-illness-conclave-holy-see-health-crisis.php, accessed 23 June 2025, quoting Javier Martínez-Brocal, *Conclave: Rules for Electing the Next Pope. Updated with the Latest Changes* (Amazon Digital Services, 2025).

[3] Holy See Press Office, "Information for Journalists," May 6, 2025.

[4] John L. Allen, Jr., "Under Consideration: Profiles of Papal Candidates," *National Catholic Reporter* (April 15, 2005), 18.

⁵ Marecellino D'Ambrosio, "Ressourcement Theology, Aggiornamento, and the Hermeneutics of Tradition," *Communio* 18 (Winter 1991): 530–555; John F. Kobler, "On D'Ambrosio and Ressourcement Theology," *Communio* 19 (Summer 1992): 321–325.

⁶ Allen, "Under Consideration: Profiles of Papal Candidates," 18.

⁷ John L. Allen, Jr., "An American Pope Is Not Likely, But...," *National Catholic Reporter* (April 7, 2005), https://www.nationalcatholicreporter.org/update/conclave/pt040705a.htm, accessed 25 June 2025.

⁸ *College of Cardinals Report*, "Cardinal Pietro Parolin," https://collegeofcardinalsreport.com/cardinals/pietro-parolin/, accessed 25 June 2025.

⁹ Gerard O'Connell, "Backer of Cardinal Parolin attacks Pope Francis' push for lay involvement in church governance," *America* (April 30, 2025), https://www.americamagazine.org/faith/2025/04/30/attack-pope-francis-campaign-cardinal-parolin-250534, accessed 25 June 2025.

¹⁰ *College of Cardinals Report*, "Cardinal Matteo Maria Zuppi," https://collegeofcardinalsreport.com/cardinals/matteo-maria-zuppi/, accessed 25 June 2025.

¹¹ *College of Cardinals Report*, "Cardinal Luis Antonio Gokim Tagle," https://collegeofcardinalsreport.com/cardinals/luis-antonio-gokim-tagle/, accessed 25 June 2025.

¹² Joshua McElwee and Crispian Balmer, "Papal conclave: All cardinals who will elect a new pope arrive in Rome," *Reuters* (May 5, 2025), https://www.reuters.com/world/europe/all-cardinals-who-will-elect-new-pope-arrive-rome-ahead-conclave-2025-05-05/, accessed 25 June 2025.

¹³ *College of Cardinals Report*, "Cardinal Lazzaro You Heung-sik," https://collegeofcardinalsreport.com/cardinals/lazzaro-you-heung-sik/, accessed 25 July 2025.

¹⁴ Steven R. Harmon, *Baptists, Catholics, and the Whole Church: Partners in the Pilgrimage to Unity* (Hyde Park, NY: New City Press, 2021).

¹⁵ McElwee and Balmer, "Papal conclave."

CHAPTER 6
CONCLAVE DAY ONE

The conclave to select the successor to Pope Francis commenced on Wednesday afternoon, May 7. At 10:00 that morning, Cardinal Giovanni Battista Re, dean of the College of Cardinals, led a public Mass "Pro Eligendo Pontifice" ("For the Election of the Pontiff") in St. Peter's Basilica. He concluded his homily with prayers "that the Holy Spirit … will give us a new Pope according to God's heart for the good of the Church and of humanity" and "will enlighten the minds of the Cardinal electors and help them agree on the Pope that our time needs."[1]

CONVERSATIONS WITH ECUMENICAL FRIENDS

While the cardinals were making these liturgical preparations for entering the conclave, I was beginning my first day of the conclave by visiting two ecumenical friends at the Centro Pro Unione, an ecumenical center and library in central Rome near the Piazza Navona. I had met the current director of the Centro Pro Unione, Fr. James (Jim) Loughran, S.A. when he was director of the Graymoor Ecumenical and Interreligious Institute in Graymoor, New York. I was a member of a consultation that met there in January 2006 to examine the reasons plans for a "Second Conference on Faith and Order in North America" in 2007 that would mark the 50th anniversary the landmark 1957 North American Conference on Faith and Order in Oberlin, Ohio, ending up being abandoned, as well as to envision possibilities for moving the aims of the abandoned conference forward in other ways.[2] Fr. Jim also previously served as editor of the periodical *Ecumenical Trends*, to which I had contributed articles during his tenure as editor.[3]

Teresa Rossi, the associate director of the Centro Pro Unione, was a member of the Catholic delegation to the joint commission for Phase II of the international ecumenical dialogue between the Baptist World Alliance and the Catholic Church that met 2006–2010, for which I was a member of the Baptist delegation. An important aspect of these dialogues is the forming of ecumenical friendships between dialogue partners that continue beyond the working sessions of the dialogue. These friendships are both expressions of the Christian unity toward which we are working and means of facilitating the reception of the results of dialogue among the churches we represent. It was good to have the opportunity to renew friendships with these two ecumenical friends while in Rome to cover the conclave.

They agreed to provide brief interviews for me to share with readers of Good Faith Media, which I am summarizing and quoting here. I filmed their responses, which were incorporated into a video shared by Good Faith Media on its YouTube channel.[4]

I asked Fr. Jim to offer a brief "elevator conversation" summary of how the Centro Pro Unione came into being and what it seeks to accomplish. He explained, "The Centro Pro Unione is a ministry of the Franciscan Friars of the Atonement, which is an American congregation of Franciscans based in Graymoor, New York." (The initials "S.A." after Fr. Jim's name indicate that the Franciscan Friars of the Atonement, also known as the Society of the Atonement, is the religious order to which he belongs.)

He said that it was "established in 1967 right after the Second Vatican Council. It was here that the non-Catholic observers to the Second Vatican Council met every week during the sessions of the council. So, it's an historically ecumenical location." He also told me that the floor above the space that the center now occupies in the building was where the ecumenical observers had their lodgings during the years of the council (1962–1965).

Fr. Jim continued, "We have a vast library of over 30,000 volumes dedicated to the ecumenical movement, so we are a research center. We're also an education/formation institution for ecumenism. We offer lectures; we offer a summer course in ecumenism in June and July every year. We reach out to other organizations in Rome, both Catholic and other church organizations that are here, for the sake of dialogue with the Catholic Church."

Teresa had been involved in a formal expression of the dialogue that the center seeks to encourage, through the Baptist-Catholic dialogue in which we both participated. I asked her to reflect on what participating in that dialogue meant to her personally. She replied, "I think that what I have experienced in those years of Catholic-Baptist dialogue in which I have been involved…is a sense of what is really the goal of ecumenism: restoring communion among Christians by overcoming the historical distance of divisions, overcoming the theological distance of different doctrinal positions, and overcoming the affective distance—destroying prejudices, stereotypes, and building new fraternity and a new sense of unity. I have experienced all three of these aspects in my involvement with my Baptist friends and colleagues."

Teresa said, "I have also experienced a very interesting theological exercise of really thinking in a new way. Pope Paul VI wrote in his encyclical *Ecclesiam Suam* ["On the Church"] that we really have to think outside of our normal line of thinking in order to become teachers and wise people.[5] I experienced that as we were drafting our final report—the way in which we were trying to really emphasize what unites us, which we put in bold [type] in our editing of the [final] report." (Our Baptist-Catholic dialogue Phase II report, *The Word of God in the Life of the Church,* had employed bold type to set forth what we affirmed together about Scripture and its relationship to tradition, baptism and the Eucharist/Lord's Supper, Mary, and the ecclesial function of oversight, followed by paragraphs in regular type explaining the convergence and noting ongoing differences in relation to it.[6]) She continued, "But also we, at least in my opinion, created some new words to express some new concepts. So, using new words carries new memories, and this is what I think we were hoping to give to the next generation—new words of unity and new memories for the future."

Teresa's reference to the encyclical *Ecclesiam Suam* by Pope Paul VI, elected pope in the midst of the Second Vatican Council in 1963 after the death of Pope John XXXIII, who had convened the council and defined its aim as *aggiornamento,* bringing the church up to date in its engagement with the modern world (a legacy of Vatican II explained in the preceding chapter of this book), was to this section:

> [I]t becomes obvious in a dialogue that there are various ways of coming to the light of faith and it is possible to make them all converge on the same goal. However divergent these ways may be, they can often serve to complete each other. They encourage us to think on different lines. They force us to go more deeply into the subject of our investigations and to find better ways of expressing ourselves. It will be a slow process of thought, but it will result in the discovery of elements of truth in the opinion of others and make us want to express our teaching with great fairness. It will be set to our credit that we expound our doctrine in such a way that others can respond to it, if they will, and assimilate it gradually. It will make us wise; it will make us teachers.[7]

I have experienced along with Teresa through our shared experience of dialogue between Baptists and Catholics this "discovery of elements of truth in the opinion of others" and increased desire "to express our teaching with great fairness." I trust that this has indeed helped us grow in wisdom and in our capacity for teaching more fully the way of Jesus Christ.

Since we were having this conversation in the context of the conclave to elect a new pope, I asked Fr. Jim if he might share his perspective on why the office of the papacy might be significant even for non-Catholic Christians. He said, "The Bishop of Rome, the Pope, has a ministry—from the beginning, we Catholics understand—to work for the unity of the church, to be a kind of preacher ... for the unity of the church." He added, "This is becoming more and more appreciated by non-Catholic Christians, our brothers and sisters in other churches who do see a significant role for a church leader to be someone who can convoke a gathering of Christians, who can be…at least symbolically a presence for the unity of the church."

As I was filming Fr. Jim's response, I smiled behind the camera at his mention of "our brothers and sisters in other churches." Despite the ecumenical advances of Vatican II, among them the recognition in its Decree on Ecumenism *Unitatis Redintegratio* (literally, "the repair of unity") that non-Catholic followers of Jesus Christ are "separated" brothers and sisters "who believe in Christ and have been truly baptized are in communion with the Catholic Church even though this communion is imperfect,"[8] the technical language of Catholic ecclesiology reserves the designation "church" for the Catholic Church and for other churches that have maintained the historic episcopate (apostolic succession in the ordination of bishops and those whom bishops ordain) and common convictions regarding the eucharistic mystery, in particular the Eastern Orthodox churches. "Ecclesial communities" is the Catholic designation for the various Protestant communities of Christians that do not fully share these elements of church regarded as essential to the fullness of church in Catholic understanding, but which nevertheless do embody important aspects of Christian faith and practice within their own communions. (This does suggest that there is at least a "churchiness" about a Baptist congregation, for example, in Catholic perspective.)

The exclusion of Protestants from this technical definition of "church" became an especially sore point in the wake of a document issued by the Catholic Church's Congregation for the Doctrine of the Faith in 2000, "Declaration '*Dominus Iesus*' on the Unicity and Salvific Universality of Jesus Christ and the Church."[9] That document had maintained that "the ecclesial communities which have not preserved the valid Episcopate and the genuine and integral substance of the Eucharistic mystery, are not Churches in the proper sense [*in sensu proprio*]."[10] Some of us excluded by that definition have found somewhat helpful the explanation offered by Catholic dialogue partners that the language in question, "in the proper sense"—"*in sensu proprio*" in the document's original Latin—means something like "in the sense that is proper to us," that is, in the sense of the distinctively Catholic understanding of the essence of the church. Thus, it may have been intended more as a word of internal theological clarification rather than an external word of exclusion.[11] Nevertheless, when I heard Fr. Jim refer to non-Catholic Christians as "our brothers and sisters in other churches," I was grateful that this particular Catholic theologian had implicitly called my own Baptist ecclesial community a "church." It would not be the last time during the next few days that I would rejoice at the use of this language.

THE CONCLAVE BEGINS

After my morning conversation with these ecumenical friends, I made the mile walk to Vatican City to resume coverage of the conclave. There was no press briefing on Wednesday, as on Tuesday the cardinals had concluded their daily congregation meetings and there were no new developments to report. Most of the members of the press corps worked in the Holy See Press Office briefing room while watching video monitors showing the Vatican's live video feed of the cardinal's activities at the beginning the conclave prior to being locked into the Sistine Chapel and their living quarters at the Casa Santa Maria, sealed off from contact with the outside world. (The word "conclave" is from a Latin word spelled the same way, which means "with key." The practice of locking the cardinals in for the conclave began in 1271, when local citizenry, impatient with the cardinals' inability to choose a pope during the three years that had elapsed since the death of Pope Clement IV in 1268, locked them into the Papal Palace in the city of Viterbo north of Rome and reduced their rations to hasten their decision making. In 1274 Pope Gregory X, whom they elected, established the rules governing papal conclaves that are observed to this day.)

At 4:00 p.m. we saw the cardinals assemble for prayer in the Pauline Chapel, near the Sistine Chapel in the Vatican complex. Then they processed to the Sistine Chapel while chanting in Latin the "Litany of the Saints," which invites the prayers of around a hundred named saints from across the history of the church (for example, *Sancte Augustine / ora pro nobis*, "Saint Augustine / pray for us").[12] I found this extended invocation of representatives of the larger communion of saints, the "great cloud of witnesses" (Hebrews 12:1) with which we are joined when we pray and engage in other acts of worship, deeply moving. Once they were all in the Sistine Chapel, one-by-one in order of seniority the cardinals swore their oath of secrecy with a hand placed on the Gospel book. The oath they swore in Latin is translated into English, "And I, [first name] Cardinal [last name], do so promise, pledge, and swear," and then after placing his hand on the Gospel book, "So help me God and these Holy Gospels which I touch with my hand."

A couple of weeks after my return from Rome from covering the conclave, I was a panelist for a special session on the new pope during the joint annual meeting of the College Theology Society, a Catholic academic organization, and the National Association of Baptist Professors of Religion Region at Large at the University of Dayton (founded by members of the

Society of Mary order). One of my fellow panelists, a Catholic theologian, shared with us the experience of watching on television the cardinals' procession into the Sistine Chapel with his young sons, who were enthralled by the bright crimson vestments and the liturgical choreography they were witnessing. They took delight in the name of one of the cardinals, Cardinal (Pierbattista) Pizzaballa, the Latin Patriarch of Jerusalem. One of his sons asked, "Where are the girls?" I found it significant that his son's young experiences of Catholic spaces in American Catholicism, despite an all-male priesthood, was gender-inclusive enough that a chapel full of only men seemed unusual to him. And this Baptist advocate for the full inclusion of women in all aspects of the life of the church again smiled.

When all cardinal electors had sworn their oath, master of ceremonies Archbishop Diego Ravelli declared, "*Extra omnes*!" ("Everybody out!"), directing everyone not a cardinal elector (cardinals under the age of 80) or essential staff to leave. At a restaurant table adjacent to mine during my dinner that evening, I overheard a journalist suggest to a colleague that the master of ceremonies' tone of voice communicated, "Get the f____ out!" At 5:46 p.m., the doors were shut and locked, sealing the conclave off from the outside world, and in that outside world our waiting began. Inside the Sistine Chapel, Cardinal Pietro Parolin, Vatican Secretary of State, began presiding over the conclave as the most senior member of the College of Cardinals under 80. A single initial round of voting was scheduled for Wednesday. Then, assuming they have not elected a pope by two-thirds majority in this first round, they would retire to the secure conclave living quarters at Casa Santa Maria for the night. Up to four rounds of voting would be held on each subsequent day until they succeeded in electing a pope.

Gerard O'Connell, *America* magazine associate editor and Vatican correspondent who authored the definitive history of the 2013 conclave that elected Pope Francis,[13] explained in a video clip from a recording of an episode of America Media's "Inside the Vatican" conclave podcast that the first vote on the morning after the evening initial vote is a crucial one, because the cardinals have had the night in between to reflect on the pattern of the one vote on the first day and to think about whether they might vote differently in light of it—for example, recognizing that their first preference didn't generate enough votes the first time to be viable in subsequent rounds, so they may need to shift their support to someone who has the likelihood of gaining additional support who might represent what they want in the future pope. He said that there is wisdom in having only one round of voting on the first day for that reason.[14]

WAITING FOR THE SMOKE

After the beginning of that first voting session, many of us in the press corps had dinner and then returned to St. Peter's Square to wait for the first issue of smoke from the chimney above the Sistine Chapel (to the right of the dome of St. Peter's Basilica when facing the basilica). Vatican Media estimated that about 45,000 of us were packed into the square, extending into the Via della Conciliazione, the central street that leads to the square. We had been told that an approximate time for seeing the smoke after the first ballot might be 7:00–8:00 p.m. In 2013, that occurred at 7:40 p.m. This time around, that time came and went and extended through the 8:00 p.m. hour, until at 9:00 p.m. black smoke billowed from the chimney. One reason for the delay might have been that there were more cardinals voting than were eligible to vote in the 2013 conclave. They cast their ballots into an urn one at a time, and then they are carefully counted, and the results announced. It was also noted that Cardinal Raniero Cantalamessa, who delivered a meditation inside the locked and sealed Sistine Chapel before the voting began, delivered an extra-long homily that might have accounted for some of the additional time taken in this first session. It would seem that the experience of long-winded preaching on occasion may be yet something else shared in common by Baptists and Catholics.

When I exited the Via della Conciliazione and turned onto the Corso Vittorio Emanuele II to cross the Tiber River on my walk back to my guest room that night, I encountered a young man from East Timor who had just arrived in Rome from London where he was living. He asked my advice on the best place nearby to wait for a taxi. His name was Francis, and he told me how he wanted to be in Rome to witness the election of the successor of Pope Francis, who had been a great inspiration to his own Catholic faith and with whom he shared a name (his parents had named him for Saint Francis of Assisi). My conversation with this brother in Christ from East Timor by way of London about our shared faith, our mutual appreciation for Pope

Francis, and our hopes for a new pope reminded me of one of the senses in which the church is "catholic," the church that is "according to the whole" (the basic meaning of the Greek word *katholikē*). In the fourth century, the church father Cyril of Jerusalem had explained in one of his catechetical lectures that "the Church is called Catholic because it is spread throughout the world, from end to end of the earth."[15] My encounter with Francis on the street in Rome was a manifestation of the geographical catholicity of the Catholic Church, which is indeed spread throughout the whole world, but also of the geographical catholicity of the whole church that includes the Catholic Church but is not limited to it.

NOTES

[1] Cardinal Giovanni Battista Re, "Holy Mass 'Pro Eligendo Pontifice,' Homily," May 7, 2025, https://www.vatican.va/content/vatican/en/special/sede-vacante/sede-vacante-2025/20250507-omelia-proeligendo-pontifice.html, accessed 25 June 2025.

[2] "A Call to the Churches for a Second Conference on Faith and Order in North America," in *Faith and Order: Toward a North American Conference. Study Guide*, ed. Norman A. Hjelm (Grand Rapids, Mich.: William B. Eerdmans, 2004), 3–11. Lutheran theologian Robert W. Jenson, who also participated in the Graymoor consultation, offered this perspective on the reasons for the failure of the proposed conference: "It was undone by mainline Protestantism's present indifference to and distraction from the whole matter, by evangelicalism's unconcern about separation at the Lord's table, and by deliberate obstruction from within the established ecumenical apparatus" (Robert W. Jenson, "God's Time, Our Time: An Interview with Robert W. Jenson," *Christian Century* 123, no. 9 [May 2, 2006]: 33).

[3] Steven R. Harmon, "Ecumenical Theology and/as Systematic Theology," *Ecumenical Trends* 38, no. 9 (October 2009): 6/134-9/137, 15/143; idem, "How Baptists Receive the Gifts of Catholics and Other Christians," *Ecumenical Trends* 39, no. 6 (June 2010): 1/81–5/85.

[4] Steven R. Harmon, James Loughran, and Teresa Ross, "Ecumenical Voices Ahead of the Papal Conclave," *Good Faith Media* (May 8, 2025), https://youtu.be/LWwM_Cb7-IA?feature=shared, accessed 26 June 2025.

[5] Pope Paul VI, *Ecclesiam Suam* (Encyclical "On the Church"), August 6, 1964, https://www.vatican.va/content/paul-vi/en/encyclicals/documents/hf_p-vi_enc_06081964_ecclesiam.html, accessed 26 June 2025.

[6] Baptist World Alliance and Catholic Church, *The Word of God in the Life of the Church: A Report of International Conversations Between the Catholic Church and the Baptist World Alliance, 2006-2010* (Falls Church, VA: Baptist World Alliance, 2013), https://baptistworld.org/wp-content/uploads/2021/01/Baptist-Catholic-Dialogue-Phase-II.pdf, accessed 26 June 2025.

[7] Pope Paul VI, *Ecclesiam Suam*, § 83.

[8] Second Vatican Council, *Unitatis Redintegratio* (Decree on Ecumenism), November 21, 1964, § 3, https://www.vatican.va/archive/hist_councils/ii_vatican_council/documents/vat-ii_decree_19641121_unitatis-redintegratio_en.html, accessed 26 June 2025.

[9] Congregation for the Doctrine of the Faith, "Declaration '*Dominus Iesus*' on the Unicity and Salvific Universality of Jesus Christ and the Church," https://www.vatican.va/roman_curia/congregations/cfaith/documents/rc_con_cfaith_doc_20000806_dominus-iesus_en.html, accessed 26 June 2025.

[10] Ibid., § 17.

[11] I explain more fully the Catholic distinction between "churches" and "ecclesial communities" and its implications in Steven R. Harmon, *Baptists, Catholics, and the Whole Church: Partners in the Pilgrimage to Unity* (Hyde Park, NY: New City Press, 2021), 31–33.

[12] *Litaniae Sanctorum* ("Litany of the Saints"), https://www.preces-latinae.org/thesaurus/Sancti/LitSanctorum.html, accessed 26 June 2025.

[13] Gerard O'Connell, *The Election of Pope Francis: An Inside Account of the Conclave That Changed History* (Maryknoll, NY: Orbis Books, 2019).

[14] America Media, Instagram reel, May 7, 2025, https://www.instagram.com/reel/DJXIq8MPLtU/?igsh=M3hud3RwNGsxYzYz, accessed 26 June 2025.

[15] Cyril of Jerusalem *Catecheses* 18.23, in *The Works of Saint Cyril of Jerusalem*, trans. Leo P. McCauley and Anthony A. Stephenson (Fathers of the Church, vol. 64; Washington, DC: The Catholic University of America Press, 1970), 2:132.

Chapter 7

Conclave Day Two: White Smoke!

The cardinals resumed their voting at 9:00 a.m. on Thursday, May 8. This time the press pool largely worked inside the Holy See Press Office briefing room while glancing now and then at the "chimney cam" feed on large video monitors at the front of the room. At about 11:50 a.m., we again had black smoke. As the plans were for there to be two rounds of voting in the morning and two rounds in the afternoon and for smoke to be released only after each two rounds of voting (unless the first round in the pair of rounds succeeds in electing a pope), this meant that the cardinals had managed to complete two rounds of voting in less than the time taken for the single round of voting on Wednesday evening.

Voting Enters Round Four

After lunch, I worked throughout the afternoon in the Holy See Press Office briefing room while waiting for the smoke that would signal the outcome of the afternoon voting rounds. A few minutes after 6:00 p.m., I looked up at the "chimney cam" on the video monitors when it sounded like there were cheers coming from the crowd in St. Peter's Square. It was a false alarm. There were jumbo video monitors in the square also displaying the feed from the camera on the roof of the Sistine Chapel, and it had become customary for the crowd to cheer when one of the "Holy See-gulls," as some of us had dubbed them, alighted beside the chimney. The crowd cheered especially enthusiastically whenever a seagull chick appeared on camera, and in this case a whole seagull family was temporarily the star of the show: presumably a mother, father, and their chick. I knew that my wife Kheresa would enjoy seeing this, so I took a photo of the screen to text to her. Before I could send the text, there was another cheering sound in the square, this time louder. We all looked up at the screen to see not only the little seagull family but wisps of white smoke rising from the chimney and swirling around the seagulls. I heard a group of journalists working around a table in an adjoining room exclaim, "Biana! Bianca!" ("White! White!"). It was 6:08 p.m.

We all leapt to our feet, grabbed gear (while I had a stabilizing frame and external microphone with me, I had time only to take my phone), and streamed out of the Holy See Press Office onto the Via della Conciliazione toward the square. Midway up the briefing room aisle, I made a video call to Kheresa and shouted when she answered, "We have white smoke!" When I made it outside, I switched the camera to front view so she could see the white smoke for herself.

Back in North Carolina where Kheresa was at work in Charlotte as Minister for Children and Their Families at St. John's Baptist Church, it was 12:08 p.m. Later in the day, she shared to Facebook her experience of receiving the call:

> Normally my lunch travels with me to church. It stayed home today, so off to Cedar Land Restaurant & Specialty Grocery I went. As soon as my hand reached to open the market's door, a request to FaceTime with Steve stopped me. I answered and he screamed, "White smoke! We have white smoke!" For a split second, I watched as white smoke puffed out of the chimney. Steve began running and the call ended. What did I do this afternoon on Central Avenue? I screamed, "We have a pope! We have a pope!" I got some looks, so I went inside the Halal market to grab my lentils (of course!). Could I keep my mouth shut? Of course not! I proclaimed the good news of great joy to everyone in there. I'm sure their lives were changed forever by this crazy, enthusiastic woman with a bowl of lentil soup.[1]

My phone connection with Kheresa was dropped when I moved beyond Holy See Press Office Wi-Fi range to the street, which was barricaded due both to the creation of a pathway for pilgrims to the Holy Door at St. Peter's Basilica throughout the 2025 Jubilee Year and the events from the funeral of Pope Francis through the conclave. To get phone video footage of me reporting on the white smoke with the sight of a smoky St. Peter's Square and the sound of pealing bells in the background for Good Faith Media, I jumped a couple of barricades (the press badge lets one get away with a lot in Vatican City) and made it into the middle of the street leading into the square. I recorded a quick video, jumped back over one barricade, and slid under another, and ran back into the press briefing room to get a Wi-Fi signal to get the video uploaded to my editors.

WAITING TO LEARN THE NEW POPE'S IDENTITY

Most of the journalists returned to the briefing room, where we had both a Wi-Fi signal and a Vatican video and audio feed that would allow us to see and hear what happens next, including especially being able to discern the identity of the new pope when presented on the balcony much better than could most of the crowd in St. Peter's Square. The following is my close-to-live written reporting on what we learned as we learned it. At 7:06 p.m., I began writing close-to-live reporting on the events leading to the presentation of the new pope to the public so that Good Faith Media could publish a story online soon thereafter.

Before I began writing the story, on the briefing room monitors we saw uniformed marching bands parading into the front portion of the square immediately in front of the steps leading up to St. Peter's Basilica, accompanied by members of the colorfully attired Swiss Guard.

At 7:12 p.m., we saw people emerge through red curtains onto the Loggia of Blessings, the central balcony of St. Peter's Basilica. Cardinal Dominique Mamberti, the Protodeacon of the College of Cardinals, declared in Latin: "Annuntio vobis gaudium magnum: Habemus Papam! Eminentissimum ac reverendissimum Dominum, Dominum Robertum Franciscum Prevost, Sanctae Romanae Ecclesiae Cardinalem Prevost, qui sibi nomen imposuit Leo XIV." In English: "I announce to you with great joy: We have a Pope! Most Eminent and Most Reverend Lord, Sir Robert Francis, Cardinal of the Holy Roman Church, Prevost, who has taken the name of Leo XIV." At the name "Prevost," there was a collective gasp in the press room punctuated by exclamations of "American!" followed by the sound of furious keyboarding as we worked on getting our initial stories filed as quickly as possible.

The cardinals had indeed elected an American pope: Cardinal Robert Prevost from the United States, born in Chicago. Biographical information was readily available once we heard the name, as Prevost had been mentioned in some of the pre-conclave stories on the *papabili*, though not in their shortlists of the top three or four possibilities. An exception was National Catholic Reporter Vatican correspondent Christopher White, who on April 30 had published a story on Prevost titled "The first American pope? This cardinal has the best chance of making history in this conclave."[2] We soon learned that on May 6, the day before the conclave began, American nun Sister Rose Pacatte, F.S.P. (Daughters of Saint Paul) had encountered CBS News senior correspondent Norah O'Donnell in St. Peter's Square and granted her an interview. When O'Donnell asked Pacatte who among the 133 cardinals in the conclave she thought might best advance the cause of women in the Catholic Church if elected pope, Pacatte immediately mentioned Prevost.[3] (The Daughters of Saint Paul, I learned, are known as the "Media Nuns" for their dedication to the apostolate of publishing and media.) In other words, the election of Prevost was not completely unforeseen, but we had so absorbed the common wisdom that an American would never be elected pope (largely because of mistrust of American exercises of power in the world)—which we learned that Prevost himself had quoted to friends prior to the conclave to assure them that he would not be elected—that we were shocked along with the rest of the world.

We went to work summarizing the basic biographical details for our media outlets, knowing that in the coming days we'd continue to discover pertinent information that would contextualize Prevost's election and suggest insights into its significance for the future of the Catholic Church. He was already working in Rome as Prefect for the Dicastery for Bishops, a position to which Pope Francis had appointed him in 2023. He had an extensive ministerial background as a missionary: he began serving as a priest in Peru in 1985 and returned there in 1988 following his doctoral studies in canon law at the Pontifical University of St. Thomas Aquinas (the "Angelicum") in Rome to serve in a variety of ministerial, administrative, and academic roles, including a decade serving as a seminary professor of canon law, patristics, and moral theology. In 2015, Pope Francis sent Prevost back to Peru as a bishop, a role in which he served until 2023, when he became Prefect of the Dicastery for Bishops. In his identification with the Peruvian people he served, Prevost had become a dual Peruvian and American citizen, so we began qualifying the headline that Prevost had become the first American pope. He is the first pope from North America, the second pope with citizenship in a South American country, and the first pope whose citizenship is in the Americas, plural.

Like Pope Francis, Prevost belonged to a religious order—Francis was a Jesuit, and Prevost was an Augustinian—the same order to which Martin Luther had belonged when he set the Protestant Reformation in motion. He served as Prior General for the Augustinians from 2001 to 2013, based in Rome but traveling frequently to a total of 47 countries in his role as head of the Augustinian order. During that time, he enjoyed making some of these trips driving himself by car, including one road trip through Germany with stops to visit sites connected with Luther the sixteenth-century Augustinian.[4]

Hearing that Prevost had taken the papal name Leo XIV set everyone to searching for details about the last pope to bear that name and speculating about Prevost's reasons for choosing it. Pope Leo XIII was pope from 1878 to 1903. While we were waiting for Pope Leo XIV to be presented to the public on the loggia and make his first remarks as pope, fellow Baptist theologian Andy Black, who did his doctoral studies in theology at the Catholic-affiliated University of Dayton, posted this on my Facebook timeline: "Haven't seen it mentioned yet, but my first thought is to ask whether 'Leo' is a nod to the most recent Leo (XIII), the originator of modern Catholic Social Teaching, who spoke to the crises of political economy created by industrialization and early 'globalization'." Others were quickly arriving at the same conclusion regarding the connections, noting in particular Leo XIII's 1891 encyclical *Rerum Novarum*, "On Capital and Labor," which addressed the harm done to humanity and in particular workers by the modern industrial revolution and, as Andy Black noted in his Facebook post, is regarded as the key document in the origination of Catholic social teaching.[5]

According to a preview article of the *papabili* published by CBS News before the conclave, "While Prevost is seen overall as a centrist, on some key social issues he's viewed as progressive. He has long embraced marginalized groups, a lot like Francis, who championed migrants and the poor."[6] According to that piece, he also opposed ordaining women as deacons. But it should be noted that Pope Francis opposed doing so, too. On May 8, there were clear signs that on a wide range of issues the new pope would continue moving along the path of Pope Francis, but there was also much that was unknown about the specific directions Pope Leo XIV would take this trajectory in the life of the Catholic Church.

THE NEW POPE SPEAKS

At 7:23 p.m., Pope Leo XIV appeared on the balcony in white alb, scarlet cape, and ruby red and gold stole—returning to the traditional accompaniments to the plain white alb that Pope Francis had intentionally worn without the additions of cape and stole when he was presented on the loggia in 2013. Pope Leo was smiling and waving to the crowd. He addressed the crowd in what seemed to be impeccable Italian. (Impeccability is a Catholic ecclesial thing, so the pun may be regarded as intended.) Not speaking or understanding Italian myself, I would have to wait for the Vatican to post an English translation to know what he said. At 7:32 p.m., he shifted into Spanish and seemed to be speaking of his time as a missionary bishop in Peru. (A journalist observed to me that weekend that the new pope's Italian was spoken with a Spanish—rather than American English—accent, owing to his time in Peru.) By 7:37 p.m., he had finished speaking, and as the crowd in St. Peter's Square cheered wildly, he was visibly moved and fighting back tears.

Between the conclusion of Pope Leo's first address and the press briefing we anticipated was coming, I was interviewed on an Irish radio station for a reaction to the election of an American pope from an American in Rome. Another journalist and I had observed that the hand dryer in the briefing room washroom was no longer working and were joking that we had broken it covering the conclave, and he realized that I had an American accent and asked if he could interview me for his station in Ireland. We stepped outside to record the interview on the sidewalk in front of the press office.

Unfortunately, I did not write down the name of the station, but I know that it was not RTÉ. I trust that someone somewhere in Ireland heard my interview.

At 8:55 p.m., Holy See Press Office Director Matteo Bruni entered the briefing room to update us on the events of the afternoon. He pointed out that Pope Leo XIV's first words were words of peace—a peace that is "unarmed and disarming." Leo gave a blessing that repeated the last message of Pope Francis on Easter Sunday hours before his death: "God cares for us, He loves you all, and evil will not prevail." Bruni confirmed that the name Leo XIV was chosen precisely because of the connection with Leo XIII's role in shaping the tradition of Catholic Social Teaching, in particular through his 1891 encyclical *Rerum Novarum*. Bruni said, "In this context, it is clearly a reference to the lives of men and women, to their work—even in an age marked by artificial intelligence."[7]

Bruni told us that Pope Leo would next appear publicly on Sunday, May 11, at noon to lead the people in St. Peter's Square in the Regina Caeli prayer (an antiphon addressed to the Blessed Virgin Mary during Eastertide) from the loggia (central balcony) of St. Peter's Basilica. He also extended to us the invitation to participate in an audience that Pope Leo XIV will hold with journalists who have been in Rome to cover the funeral of Pope Francis and the papal conclave in the Paul VI Audience Hall on Monday, May 12, at 10:00 a.m.

At 9:30 p.m., my fellow journalists in the press room still had not called it a day, continuing to write and research and communicate with sources, colleagues, and editors. But I had not eaten since 1:00 p.m. and needed nourishment, so I packed up and headed to my favorite Vatican City restaurant, Il Wine Bar De' Penitenzieri on Borgo Santo Spirito, which I had frequented enough to be adopted as a regular by a waiter named Christian, who gave me a gratis dessert or digestif more than once when a busy restaurant made service slower than usual. Christian was working again that night, and I said to him, "We have a pope!" He said, "Yes, I was surprised. An American!" I surmised that he wasn't sure that would be a good thing.

A couple of days after my May 14 departure from Rome, I read an article by Cathleen Falsani, who arrived in Rome on Sunday after the election of the new pope to cover his installation for the *Chicago Sun-Times* and write stories on the connections of Chicagoans to the Chicago-born pope. Cathleen was one of my lunch companions on Monday, May 12, following Pope Leo's audience with us. Her new article highlighted the reactions of Roman Italians to the election of the "pope Americano," and I discovered that she had interviewed Christian, my favorite Roman waiter. She wrote:

> When Leo stepped out onto the central loggia of St. Peter's Basilica a week ago, Christian Luciani, 55, a waiter at De' Penitenzieri restaurant just a few blocks away, was "absolutely surprised" that he was an American.
>
> "But some people tell me he's very similar to the ex-pope, Franceso, and I loved him," Luciani said … "To me, he was …" Luciani said, pantomiming someone reaching out and pulling another person close. "There was no distance with him. It was incredible" …
>
> Leo "takes after Pope Francis in this way … He's not American like your president now," Luciani said, referring to Donald Trump. "I am hopeful … A long time ago we had popes who were purely political. And a political pope is not good."[8]

It was clear at the end of the second day of the conclave, the day of white smoke, that many people throughout the world—and not only Catholics—were hoping that Pope Leo XIV would prove to be the sort of pope Christian Luciani hoped he would be and were seeing signs that their hopes were warranted.

NOTES

[1] Kheresa Harmon, "Normally my lunch travels with me to church," Facebook, May 8, 2025, https://www.facebook.com/share/p/1FjgoUY9mS/, accessed 2 July 2025.

[2] Christopher White, "The first American pope? This cardinal has the best chance of making history in this conclave," *National Catholic Reporter* (April 30, 2025), https://www.ncronline.org/vatican/vatican-news/papal-front-runner-interest-polyglot-us-cardinal-prevost-rises-italian, accessed 27 June 2025.

[3] CBS News (@cbsnews) and Norah O' Donnell (@norahodonnell), "Sister Rose Pacatte, a nun for nearly 60 years, was excited when she saw CBS News' @NorahODonnell reporting in Rome for the conclave," Instagram, May 6, 2025, https://www.instagram.com/cbsnews/reel/DJZQgIoxxfV/, accessed 27 June 2025.

[4] Jason Horowitz, Julie Bosman, Elizabeth Dias, Ruth Graham, Simon Romero, and Mitra Taj, "Long Drives and Short Homilies: How Father Bob Became Pope Leo," *The New York Times*

(May 17, 2025), https://www.nytimes.com/2025/05/17/world/europe/robert-prevost-pope-leo-xiv.html, accessed 27 June 2025.

[5] Pope Leo XIII, *Rerum Novarum* ("On Capital and Labor"), May 15, 1891, https://www.vatican.va/content/leo-xiii/en/encyclicals/documents/hf_l-xiii_enc_15051891_rerum-novarum.html, accessed 27 June 2025.

[6] Anna Matranga and Frank Andrews, "Who will be the next pope? Here's a list of some possible candidates to succeed Pope Francis," *CBS News* (updated May 8, 2025), https://www.cbsnews.com/news/who-will-be-the-next-pope-list-of-possible-candidates/, accessed 27 June 2025.

[7] Francesca Merlo, "Matteo Bruni: Pope Leo XIV's name choice highlights the Church's mission," *Vatican News* (May 8, 2025), https://www.vaticannews.va/en/vatican-city/news/2025-05/matteo-bruni-holy-see-press-office-conference-leo-xiv-pope-elect.html, accessed 27 June 2025.

[8] Cathleen Falsani, "'Pray for the new pope Americano': Italians warm to Chicago-born Pope Leo as merch hits Rome streets," *Chicago Sun-Times* (May 16, 2025), https://chicago.suntimes.com/pope-leo-xiv/2025/05/16/pope-leo-robert-prevost-americano-rome-vatican-italian-for-sale, accessed 27 June 2025.

Chapter 8
Early Answers to Pre-Conclave Questions

Chapter 5 of this book addressed the question, "Who Might Become Pope?" On Friday, May 9, we began the day with the answer to that question and learned more with each passing hour. Robert Francis Prevost, age 69, born in Chicago, cardinal serving as prefect of the Dicastery for Bishops and previously in ministry roles in Peru that culminated in service as archbishop, was elected by the college of cardinals as pope in the third round of voting (and fourth round of voting overall) on Thursday, the afternoon of the second day of the conclave, and took the papal name Pope Leo XIV.

As everyone writing about Pope Leo XIV had noted in stories published Thursday evening and Friday morning, his election represented multiple "firsts": first pope from the United States, first pope with Peruvian citizenship, first pope from North America (but the second from the Americas), first pope whose first language is English, and more.

The Theological Education of Pope Leo XIV

From the perspective of my primary vocation as a theological educator in a university-related school of divinity, I noted also that he is the first pope to be the product of an institution of undergraduate higher education in the United States—Villanova University, where he studied mathematics and philosophy, along with Latin and Hebrew taken as elective courses. Former Villanova philosophy professor John D. Caputo posted on Facebook Thursday evening that the new pope was one of his students in his course on "German Existentialism and Phenomenology" in 1977.[1]

I was also struck with the realization that he is the first pope to have graduated from an institution accredited by the Association of Theological Schools in the United States and Canada, the Catholic Theological Union in Chicago. He earned a Master of Divinity (and is the first pope to have earned a degree with that specific nomenclature), which is the same degree program in which my own students at Gardner-Webb University School of Divinity are enrolled. It is significant that he studied at Catholic Theological Union—which was founded in 1968 shortly after the Second Vatican Council and sought to form students in that council's vision for the future of the Catholic Church—in part because its student body included not only candidates for the priesthood but also laypersons, and women among them. He is the only pope to date to have received his academic ministerial formation in this manner alongside laypersons and women in particular. Catholic Theological Union President Barbara Reid, a specialist in the feminist interpretation of Scripture who had once hoped to recruit Robert Prevost to serve on her faculty as a professor of canon law, gave an interview for a newspaper article in which she spoke to the significance of this aspect of Pope Leo's seminary formation:

> "Another thing that still today sets CTU apart is that from early on, women were in class right alongside the [male] seminarians," Reid said. So, [Pope Leo] would have studied right alongside women who were also doing the same degree that he was doing, and he would have had women professors."
>
> In fact, when Pope Leo was a student at CTU, his spiritual director—in the Catholic tradition, a person who is specially trained to accompany others on their spiritual journeys and in deepening a relationship with God—was a woman: Sister Lyn Osiek.
>
> A religious sister of the Sacred Heart of Jesus, Osiek was a professor of New Testament at CTU for 26 years and is a leading authority on the role of women in the early church.
>
> "For a seminarian to have a woman as spiritual director would be unheard of in other kinds of seminaries," Reid said. "So, he would have been formed in such a way that he'd be very comfortable with

women in ministry alongside him. And that's not so of all Roman Catholic seminaries and schools of theology."[2]

Furthermore, Catholic Theological Union belonged to an ecumenical consortium of Chicago-area theological seminaries that included Garrett-Evangelical Theological Seminary (Methodist), the Lutheran School of Theology at Chicago, McCormick Theological Seminary (Presbyterian), Meadville Lombard Theological School (Unitarian Universalist), North Park Theological Seminary (Evangelical Covenant), and Northern Seminary (Baptist). Students from those schools could enroll in courses at Catholic Theological Union, and students from Catholic Theological Union could enroll in courses at those other schools. This ecumenical context for Catholic theological education likely played a role in the new pope's ecumenical formation.

While he is not the only pope to have this as a previous role, Leo XIV was a seminary professor himself for a decade in Peru. Beyond his first graduate/professional theological degree, he had earned both the Licentiate of Canon Law and the Doctorate of Canon Law from the Pontifical University of St. Thomas Aquinas (the "Angelicum") in Rome.[3]

POPE LEO XIV AND THE LEGACY OF POPE FRANCIS

In Chapter 5 of this book, I raised questions about the sort of pope whom the cardinals would elect. Would he be someone who would continue the warm, open engagement of Pope Francis? There were immediate signs on Thursday evening that the answer to this question is "yes"—not necessarily in terms of personality, but in his identification with paths taken by the papacy of Francis.

The name he chose is significant in connection with the legacy of Pope Francis. Pope Leo XIII, who served as pope from 1878 until 1903, is the pope credited with launching what is now identified as "Catholic Social Teaching" with his 1891 encyclical *Rerum Novarum*, or "Rights and Duties of Capital and Labor," which was a response to the manner in which the industrial revolution at the end of the nineteenth century was harming people.[4] On Thursday evening, Vatican press director Matteo Bruni had confirmed that Leo XIV had these connections in mind when he chose his papal name. But it seems that the connection with Pope Leo XIII is also a connection with Pope Francis. In his final encyclical *Dilexit Nos*, "On the Human and Divine Love of the Heart of Jesus," published in October 2024, Pope Francis appealed to Leo XIII in a crucial sentence of the encyclical: "As my Predecessor Leo XIII pointed out, through the image of his Sacred Heart, the love of Christ 'moves us to return love for love'."[5]

By Friday morning, we had the English text of Pope Leo XIV's initial *Urbi et Orbi* ("To the City and the World") address delivered from the loggia of St. Peter's Basilica the previous evening in Italian, with a few sentences in Spanish. It suggested further connections with the legacy of Pope Francis:

> Peace be with you all!
>
> Dear brothers and sisters, these are the first words spoken by the risen Christ, the Good Shepherd who laid down his life for God's flock. I would like this greeting of peace to resound in your hearts, in your families, among all people, wherever they may be, in every nation and throughout the world. Peace be with you!
>
> It is the peace of the risen Christ. A peace that is unarmed and disarming, humble and persevering. A peace that comes from God, the God who loves us all, unconditionally.
>
> We can still hear the faint yet ever courageous voice of Pope Francis as he blessed Rome, the Pope who blessed Rome, who gave his blessing to the world, the whole world, on the morning of Easter. Allow me to extend that same blessing: God loves us, God loves you all, and evil will not prevail! All of us are in God's hands. So, let us move forward, without fear, together, hand in hand with God and with one another other! We are followers of Christ. Christ goes before us. The world needs his light. Humanity needs him as the bridge that can lead us to God and his love. Help us, one and all, to build bridges through dialogue and encounter, joining together as one people, always at peace. Thank you, Pope Francis!
>
> I also thank my brother Cardinals, who have chosen me to be the Successor of Peter and to walk together with you as a Church, united, ever pursuing peace and justice, ever seeking to act as men

and women faithful to Jesus Christ, in order to proclaim the Gospel without fear, to be missionaries.

I am an Augustinian, a son of Saint Augustine, who once said, "With you I am a Christian, and for you I am a bishop." In this sense, all of us can journey together toward the homeland that God has prepared for us.

A special greeting to the Church of Rome! Together, we must look for ways to be a missionary Church, a Church that builds bridges and encourages dialogue, a Church ever open to welcoming, like this Square with its open arms, all those who are in need of our charity, our presence, our readiness to dialogue and our love.

And if you also allow me a brief word, a greeting to everyone and in particular to my beloved Diocese of Chiclayo, in Peru, where a faithful people has accompanied its Bishop, shared its faith and given so much, so much, to continue being a faithful Church of Jesus Christ.

To all of you, brothers and sisters in Rome, in Italy, throughout the world: we want to be a synodal Church, a Church that moves forward, a Church that always seeks peace, that always seeks charity, that always seeks to be close above all to those who are suffering.[6]

I think that the connection made by the new pope's choice of a name to the legacy of Leo XIII, which was cherished by Pope Francis, combined with the echo in this initial address of Pope Francis' encouragement of communication that aims "to build bridges where many build walls,"[7] was Pope Leo XIV's way of identifying with the emphases of Pope Francis without explicitly saying so.

There were two other key terms in Leo XIV's opening address that made clear his intentions to continue on the trail blazed by Francis. One is "synodal." In Chapter 4 of this book, I identified this as a key question looming over the papal conclave: "will the successor to Pope Francis continue and implement this emphasis on the Catholic Church as a communion of discernment that listens to all voices, or will he offer qualifications or encourage redirections of the synodal path?" That question referred to the "synodal path" embarked upon through Francis' convening of the Synod on

Synodality that sought to listen to all voices within and beyond the Catholic Church in discerning how to move forward together on the path that leads to the future God desires for the church and the world.

Leo XIV declared in his address, "we want to be a synodal church, walking and always seeking peace, charity, closeness, especially to those who are suffering." While at least one cardinal speaking in the pre-conclave daily congregations of the cardinals had explicitly condemned key aspects of Francis' program of synodality, Leo XIV explicitly embraced it. "Walking" is also a key word in this context because the Synod on Synodality characterized synodality as a path on which we walk together.

A related word that stuck out in the Italian in which Leo XIV spoke was "tutti," which means "all," "everyone," or "everybody." It appears no less than twelve times in the Italian text of his address.[8] It was a favorite word of Francis, and it was a word strongly associated with his vision of a synodal path for the church as a church that includes everyone, listens to everyone, accompanies everyone, and is for everyone. The specific ways in which Pope Leo XIV will lead the Catholic Church on this path are not yet known, but his intention to do so was clearly announced in his first papal address.

Pope Leo XIV as a Writer

A further observation about the first address of Pope Leo XIV, written and delivered only an hour after his election: this pope can write! After the opening greeting "Peace be with you all!" he said this: "It is the peace of the risen Christ—a peace that is disarmed and disarming, humble and persevering; a peace that comes from God, the God who loves us all, unconditionally." (Here I've adjusted the English translation of this sentence posted on the Vatican web site to capture the parallel phraseology of the Italian in which he delivered it: "una pace disarmata e una pace disarmante."[9]) I fully expect "a peace that is disarmed and disarming" to become a defining phrase of this pontificate. This would not be the last time he would utilize it during my time in Rome.

His homiletical prose is moving through the beauty of what it calls hearers to imagine: "Together, we must look for ways to be a missionary Church, a Church that builds bridges and encourages dialogue, a Church ever open to welcoming, like this Square with its open arms, all those who are in need of our charity, our presence, our readiness to dialogue and our love."

There's also this bit of plainly articulated theological depth that references a whole body of technical ecclesiological discourse without sounding in the slightest like a theology lecture: "we want to be a synodal Church, a Church that moves forward, a Church that always seeks peace, that always seeks charity, that always seeks to be close above all to those who are suffering." I grant that "synodal" requires further explanation, but then so do a great many of the distinctive terms associated with Christian faith. But here the pope was sending a clear signal embedded in a one-word theological idiom, for those who had ears to hear what he was communicating by it.

INTERVIEWS

Twice on Friday afternoon, I switched journalistic roles from interviewer to interviewee and granted interviews from Rome to two local television stations in the United States. First, Rachel Loyd, a reporter for the local Spectrum News affiliate in Charlotte, North Carolina, who had previously interviewed me during the hospitalization of Pope Francis and again after his death, interviewed me about my experience of the conclave and presentation of Pope Leo XIV and my perspectives on the relationship of the new pope to the legacy of Pope Francis.[10] Later in the afternoon, reporter Amy Hybels from CBS 42 in Birmingham, Alabama, where I previously served on the faculty of Samford University's Beeson Divinity School, had similar questions for me and incorporated our interview into a segment on local Birmingham connections with and perspectives on the outcome of the conclave.[11] The following Monday, I granted another live radio interview to Jeff Hamlin, host of WPTF Afternoon News in Raleigh, North Carolina, who had previously interviewed me following the death of Pope Francis, this time about the election of his successor Pope Leo XIV.[12]

NOTES

[1] Jack Caputo (https://www.facebook.com/jack.caputo.79), "I'm proud to say that I had the Pope in my 'German Existentialism and Phenomenology' course in the Spring semester of his senior year (1977)," Facebook, May 8, 2025, https://www.facebook.com/share/p/15WgzndHvP/, accessed 27 June 2025.

² Cathleen Falsani, "Pope Leo XIV 'exudes kindness,' say Chicago religious leaders attending his installation in Rome," *Chicago Sun-Times* (May 17, 2025), https://chicago.suntimes.com/pope-leo-xiv/2025/05/17/pope-leo-xiv-installation-catholic-theological-union-robert-prevost-barbara-reid-john-lydon, accessed 28 June 2025.

³ Ruth Graham, Elizabeth Diaz, and Jason Horowitz, "Pope Leo's Doctoral Dissertation: Thoughts on Power and Authority," *The New York Times* (May 22, 2025), https://www.nytimes.com/2025/05/22/us/pope-leo-doctoral-dissertation.html, accessed 28 June 2025.

⁴ Pope Leo XIII, *Rerum Novarum* ("On Capital and Labor"), May 15, 1891, https://www.vatican.va/content/leo-xiii/en/encyclicals/documents/hf_l-xiii_enc_15051891_rerum-novarum.html, accessed 27 June 2025.

⁵ Pope Francis, *Dilexit Nos*, "On the Human and Divine Love of the Heart of Jesus Christ" (October 24, 2024), § 166, https://www.vatican.va/content/francesco/en/encyclicals/documents/20241024-enciclica-dilexit-nos.html, accessed 27 June 2025.

⁶ Pope Leo XIV, "First Blessing 'Urbi et Orbi' of His Holiness Pope Leo XIV," May 8, 2025, https://www.vatican.va/content/leo-xiv/en/messages/urbi/documents/20250508-prima-benedizione-urbietorbi.html, accessed 28 June 2025.

⁷ Pope Francis, "Address of His Holiness Pope Francis to the Participants in the Plenary Assembly of the Dicastery for Communication," October 31, 2024, https://www.vatican.va/content/francesco/en/speeches/2024/october/documents/20241031-dicastero-comunicazione.html, accessed 28 June 2025.

⁸ Pope Leo XIV, "Prima Benedizione 'Urbi et Orbi' del Santo Padre Leone XIV," May 8, 2025, https://press.vatican.va/content/salastampa/it/bollettino/pubblico/2025/05/08/0299/00524.html, accessed 28 June 2025.

⁹ Ibid.

¹⁰ Rachel Loyd, "N.C. professor sees similarities between Pope Leo XIV and Pope Francis," Spectrum News 1, May 9, 2025, https://spectrumlocalnews.com/nc/charlotte/news/2025/05/09/pope-leo-xiv--pope-francis--new-pope--similarities, accessed 28 June 2025.

¹¹ Amy Hybels, "Birmingham Bishop Steven Raica celebrates Mass of Thanksgiving for election of new Pope," CBS 42, May 9, 2025, https://www.cbs42.com/news/birmingham-bishop-steven-raica-celebrates-mass-of-thanksgiving-for-election-of-new-pope/, accessed 28 June 2025.

¹² Jeff Hamlin, "Steve Harmon: Gardner-Webb University Historical Theology Professor on the Current State of Affairs in the Papacy," WPTF Afternoon News, Raleigh, North Carolina, May 12, 2025, https://podcasts.apple.com/us/podcast/steve-harmon-gardner-webb-university-historical-theology/id1685263435?i=1000708187328, accessed 29 June 2025.

Chapter 9
Pope Leo XIV's First Weekend

The day after the conclusion of the conclave with the presentation of Pope Leo XIV and his first *Urbi et Orbi* message began the first weekend of his pontificate, and he chose to hit the ground running during that first weekend. His actions and words during the weekend of the Fourth Sunday in Eastertide continued to gesture toward what sort of pope he will be.

Friday, May 9

On Friday, Pope Leo XIV celebrated his first Mass—not a public Mass in St. Peter's Basilica, but a Mass for the college of cardinals in the Sistine Chapel where the previous day he had been elected by them as pope.

He delivered the homily for the Mass, and he began it be quoting the responsorial psalm from earlier in the service: "I will sing a new song to the Lord, because he has done marvels—not just with me, but with all of us." He went on to characterize the calling that the cardinals had placed on him in cruciform terms, noting that the early second-century bishop Ignatius of Antioch had come in chains to Rome as the place where he would become a martyr. He quoted from Ignatius' Letter to the Romans, in which Ignatius said, "Then I will truly be a disciple of Jesus Christ, when the world no longer sees my body," which Leo applied to what it means to exercise a ministry of authority in the church: "It is to move aside so that Christ may remain, to make oneself small so that he may be known and glorified, to spend oneself to the utmost so that all may have the opportunity to know and love him."

Leo concluded by praying that God might grant him the grace to minister in such a way.[1]

By the end of the day on Friday, *The Wall Street Journal* had already published an amazingly detailed account of the electoral dynamics inside the conclave that had concluded only the day before, titled "How an American Cardinal Beat the Odds to Become Pope."[2] It was posted at 10:34 p.m. Friday evening (Eastern Time) online and appeared in the Saturday print edition. An independently reported article in the Sunday edition of *The New York Times* corroborated many of these details under the title "How a Quiet American Cardinal Became Pope."[3]

The very short version of the story is that the first round of voting on Wednesday evening revealed that Vatican Secretary of State Cardinal Pietro Parolin, the widely acknowledged frontrunner going into the conclave, fell far short of the critical mass of votes at that stage that would indicate a viable candidacy. In informal conversations among cardinals during the pre-conclave period of the daily congregation meetings of the cardinals, Robert Prevost's name was already much-discussed in these conversations as an alternative to Parolin who would be ideologically moderate yet would continue the trajectory of the papacy of Francis, and by the third round of voting—the second voting session in the morning of the first full day of the conclave—it was apparent that the cardinals were coalescing around Prevost, and conversations during lunch seemed to confirm this direction. When the cardinals resumed voting in the fourth round overall after lunch, Prevost surged past the minimum eighty-nine votes that constituted two-thirds of the cardinal electors and reached a final tally of 105 out of 132 votes.

Cardinals who spoke to these reporters mentioned being impressed with Prevost's skills in organizing the daily congregation meetings, leading small group discussions among the cardinals, and listening deeply to people. When Prevost had his turn to deliver a brief speech in the daily congregations, he impressed his fellow cardinals not with flashy oratory but with his commitment to the vision of Pope Francis for the Catholic Church, in particular Francis' commitment to a synodal church that draws all of its members toward walking on the path toward the church's future together. As the cardinal described by some as the "least American" of the American cardinals (in the sense of "America" as a synonym for "United States of America") with deep ties of identity also to South America, Prevost drew strong support from the cardinals of the Americas, plural, as well as from the European, African, and Asian contingents.

On Friday after the Mass for the College of Cardinals in the Sistine Chapel, the cardinals from the United States granted a press conference to journalists from select media outlets at the Pontifical North American College in Rome. (The restriction of invitations to select media outlets meant that the first two questions were asked by NBC's Lester Holt, whom I later enjoyed meeting as we waited in the security line for the audience Pope Leo granted to journalists on Monday, May 12, and ABC's Terry Moran.) While I was not a part of the press pool for that conference, I was able to watch video of it later that evening. The cardinals' responses to questions provided insight into the internal dynamics of the conclave that led to the election of their colleague Robert Prevost as Pope Leo XIV, and they gave evidence of their united support for him despite the ideological differences among the U.S. cardinals.[4]

SATURDAY, MAY 10

On Saturday morning, Pope Leo XIV met with the college of cardinals. This is a customary thing for a new pope to do following his election, but this is usually mainly an address by the pope to the cardinals. Leo did speak to them, but he also wanted to engage in conversation with them to continue the dialogue about the future of the church that had begun in the pre-conclave daily congregation meetings that he had played a key role in organizing. He told them that it would be "the opportunity that many of you had asked for: a sort of dialogue with the College of Cardinals to hear what advice, suggestions, proposals, concrete things, which have already been discussed in the days leading up to the conclave."[5] According to the summary of the conversational part of the meeting provided by the Holy See Press Office, the cardinals returned to many of the themes and visions for the church that had been presented during those earlier meetings.[6]

In his address to his "brother cardinals," Leo made deliberate connections with trajectories in the Catholic Church that issue from the reforms of the Second Vatican Council (1962–1965) and in particular the way that the papacy of Pope Francis had embodied them and carried them forward. He drew from the "Apostolic Exhortation" of Francis titled *Evangelii Gaudium* ("The Joy of the Gospel") to highlight the primacy of Christ in proclamation, the missionary conversion of the entire Christian community, growth in collegiality and synodality, inclusive attention to the *sensus fidei* (the understanding of the Christian faith that belongs to the whole church, especially as expressed by piety of the faithful), loving care for the least and the rejected, and courageous and trusting dialogue with the contemporary world in its various components and realities.[7]

Leo said that he sees himself as "called to continue in this same path" (the reforms of the church in Vatican II carried forward by Pope Francis) and connected that intention to his selection of the papal name Leo XIV:

> There are different reasons for this, but mainly because Pope Leo XIII in his historic Encyclical *Rerum Novarum* addressed the social question in the context of the first great industrial revolution. In our own day, the Church offers to everyone the treasury of her social teaching in response to another industrial revolution and to developments in the field of artificial intelligence that pose new challenges for the defense of human dignity, justice and labor.[8]

This was not the only time in the first few days of Leo's papacy that he mentioned the potential threats of A.I. to human dignity and the dignity of labor. I expect one of the distinctive contributions of Pope Leo XIV to be a much-needed theological framing of artificial intelligence as a Christian ethical issue.

Later Saturday afternoon, Pope Leo visited the Shrine of the Mother of Good Counsel, which is governed by the Augustinian order that the new pope once headed. Significantly, it houses an image of the Virgin Mary that had special meaning for his predecessor Pope Leo XIII. This stop was en route to the Basilica of St. Mary Maggiore, where Pope Francis is entombed.

I had made my own pilgrimage to the tomb of Pope Francis about three hours before Pope Leo's arrival. As I stood before his simple grave (perhaps significantly, situated between two confessional booths on the side of the basilica's main worship space), I sought to put into practice something that our Baptist-Catholic dialogue agreed that Baptists and Catholics can do together in good conscience: even though all of us may not engage in the practice of the invocation of the saints—asking the saints to pray for us—we can be conscious that when we pray, we are praying along with the departed saints in the living communion of saints that includes them along with us.[9] So, I prayed along with Pope Francis. I thanked God for his life and ministry, and I prayed that I and all of us might receive more fully the way he exemplified and taught the way of Jesus. I trust that Pope Francis continues to pray for us.

When later that evening I saw the photograph released by Vatican Media of Pope Leo XIV praying at the tomb of Pope Francis, I was struck by how well this moving image captured the new pope's consciousness of indebtedness to the ministry of his predecessor and his intention to continue in the path of Francis in his own papacy.[10]

Sunday, May 11

On Sunday morning, Pope Leo delivered a brief homily in a small Mass at an altar in the crypt of the Basilica of St. Peter near the traditional tomb of Peter. In it he connected the theme of Christ the Good Shepherd Sunday to the vocation of motherhood on Mother's Day and to the vocation of pastoral ministry, encouraging his fellow ministers to encourage young people toward the vocation of ministry.[11]

At noon on Sunday, Pope Leo XIV appeared on the central balcony of the Basilica of St. Peter where he had been presented as the new pope three days earlier to lead the crowd of about 100,000 people packed into St. Peter's Square and extending into adjacent streets in the praying of the *Regina Caeli* ("Queen of Heaven"), a prayer traditionally prayed by Catholics during the season of Eastertide. He again noted the occasion of Good Shepherd Sunday, encouraged people to join him in prayer for vocations to the priesthood, and urged the church to be intentional in accompanying young people.

He returned to the call toward peace in a world torn apart by war, speaking of "a piecemeal third world war" as a threat to humanity. He mentioned specifically the war in Ukraine, calling for "an authentic, just, and lasting peace"; the devastation in the Gaza Strip, calling for an immediate ceasefire, humanitarian aid, and the freeing of hostages; and the conflict between India and Pakistan.[12] I expect peacemaking in a world of violence to be one of the distinctive emphases of Leo's papacy.

Fake Pope Leo XIV Memes

Over the weekend, memes combining photos of the new pope with quotations purportedly from Pope Leo XIV went viral on social media platforms. One meme was a photo of a bespectacled trombone player wearing a dark coat and tie who looked vaguely like Robert Prevost, accompanied by this caption:

> Vatican City, May 8, 2025 — Before ascending to the papacy as Pope Leo XIV, Robert Francis Prevost led a surprising double life: acclaimed theologian by day, and celebrated jazz trombonist by night. Known in Chicago's music circles as "Bobby Prev," he headlined several jazz festivals in the '70s and '80s with his signature mellow tone and soulful improvisations. Though he laid down the horn to follow his priestly calling, insiders say he still keeps a trombone in his Vatican apartment.

As delightful as it might be to think about the pope playing in clubs as a jazz trombonist under a different identity, there's no evidence that he did so.

Another meme that metastasized virulently online juxtaposed a photo of just-elected Pope Leo XIV waving at the crowd in St. Peter's Square from the loggia of St. Peter's Basilica, but with a somewhat severe-looking countenance, with this text:

> To all who sent prayers, love, and hope as I begin
> this sacred journey—thank you.
> I accept this role not as a throne, but as a vow:
> To serve the forgotten,
> To uplift the broken,
> To speak plainly where others stay silent.
> To be called "woke" in a world that sleeps
> through suffering is no insult—it is Gospel.
> Woke means awakened by compassion.

> Guided by truth.
> Humbled by grace.
> Committed to justice—not just for some,
> but for all.
> So let them mock.
> Let them sneer.
> We will still build the Kingdom—
> not with walls, but with love.
> Be awake. Be loving. Be woke.
> —Pope Leo XIV

As much as those of us who take being called "woke" as a compliment might be encouraged by the pope himself encouraging us to "be woke," there's no record of either Cardinal Prevost or Pope Leo saying or writing such a thing.

Another widely shared meme paired the same photo of Pope Leo XIV waving at the crowd from the balcony with these words:

> You cannot follow both Christ and the cruelty of kings.
> A leader who mocks the weak, exalts, himself, and preys on the innocent is not sent by God.
> He is sent to test you. And many are failing.
> —Pope Leo XIV

Many people might be heartened by the knowledge that Pope Leo shares their perspective on the character of the current American president and states it publicly, but alas, he did not say this.

One purported quotation in circulation was attributed variously to Robert Prevost from sometime prior to his election as pope or to Pope Leo, sometimes as a portion of his first homily as pope:

> Brothers, sisters …
> I speak to you, especially to those who no longer believe, no longer hope, no longer pray, because they think God has left.
> To those who are fed up with scandals, with misused power, with the silence of a Church that sometimes seems more like a palace than a home.

I, too, was angry with God.

I, too, saw good people die, children suffer, grandparents cry without medicine.

And yes … here were days when I prayed and only felt an echo.

But then I discovered something:

God doesn't shout. God whispers.

And sometimes He whispers from the mud, from pain, from a grandmother who feeds you without having anything.

I don't come to offer you perfect faith.

I come to tell you that faith is a walk with stones, puddles, and unexpected hugs.

I'm not asking you to believe in everything.

I'm asking you not to close the door. Give a chance to the God who waits for you without judgment.

I'm just a priest who saw God in the smile of a woman who lost her son … and yet she cooked for others.

That changed me.

So if you're broken, if you don't believe, if you're tired of the lies …

come anyway. With your anger, your doubt, your dirty backpack.

No one here will ask you for a VIP card.

Because this Church, as long as I breathe, will be a home for the homeless, and a rest for the weary.

God doesn't need soldiers.

He needs brothers.

And you, yes, you …

are one of them.

Robert Prevost (Leo XIV)

The appeal of this quotation attributed to Prevost/Leo is understandable. It did not enlist the new pope in the American culture wars. It spoke touchingly, pastorally, to the spiritual experiences of many people. But it is not an authentic quotation from Robert Prevost or Pope Leo XIV.

My favorite inauthentic Pope Leo XIV quotation meme was created by my Gardner-Webb University faculty colleague Anna Sieges Beal as a response to the viral fake quote memes and efforts in vain to stop their spread.

It superimposed the following text on a different photo of the new pope on the St. Peter's loggia, smiling broadly while waving to the crowd: "American Protestants appear so eager for a Christian leader that will say something profound about how bad Trump is that they will post pictures of me next to things I didn't say."[13] I laughed aloud, quite loudly, when I saw that Anna had tagged me in posting her meme to Facebook.

A safe assumption is that if an online search for the purported quotation doesn't yield results from the Vatican or Vatican News web sites or news stories from various outlets, it's likely not authentic, as the pope's homilies, addresses, speeches, messages, and writings are assiduously documented and made available publicly. It's also worth checking the date of a legitimate quote, as it can be important to know whether something was said or written prior to becoming pope or as the pope. But the authentic words of this gifted writer and homilist are easily findable and are worth sharing widely. I've started doing so now and then, accompanied by the hashtag #AuthenticPopeLeoXIVQuote.

A Dispatch for Italian Baptists, Methodists, and Waldensians

On the day the conclave began, I received a message from Marta D'Auria, vice president of the Baptist union in Italy and editor of *Riforma*, a weekly newspaper published by and for Baptist, Methodist, and Waldensian churches in Italy. Anticipating that the conclave would conclude with white smoke on Thursday or Friday of that week, she asked if I would be willing to contribute a commentary article of about 5,000 characters offering my perspective on the conclave and election for the front page of the following week's edition of *Riforma*, requested by Sunday evening so that she could translate it into Italian prior to publication. At the end of a weekend of covering Pope Leo XIV's first weekend as pope, I condensed my experiences of the past week, recounted at length in the present book from Chapter 3 through this point, into a little over 800 words. I concluded the original English submission with this paragraph:

> The manner in which Pope Leo XIV will follow Francis is not yet known, but his intention to do is clearly announced. If he does so,

it will benefit not only Catholics but all Christians and all people. I hope he will also help American Christians to confront injustices being done by the current administration of the USA.[14]

After I submitted my article, I drifted off to sleep anticipating the new pope's audience with journalists on Monday morning.

NOTES

[1] Pope Leo XIV, "Homily of the Holy Father Leo XIV," May 9, 2025, https://www.vatican.va/content/leo-xiv/en/homilies/2025/documents/20250509-messa-cardinali.html, accessed 28 June 2025.

[2] Stacy Meichtry, Margherita Stancati, Ian Lovett, and Marcus Walker, "How an American Cardinal Beat the Odds to Become Pope," *The Wall Street Journal* (May 9, 2025), https://www.wsj.com/world/europe/pope-leo-xiv-conclave-election-robert-prevost-0eb0f255, accessed 28 June 2025.

[3] Jason Horowitz, Emma Bubola, Elizabeth Diaz, and Patricia Mazzei, "How a Quiet American Cardinal Became Pope," *The New York Times* (May 11, 2025), https://www.nytimes.com/2025/05/11/world/europe/conclave-vote-pope-leo-robert-prevost.html, accessed 28 June 2025.

[4] Associated Press, "LIVE: US cardinals hold a press conference after Robert Prevost is named Pope Leo XIV," YouTube, May 9, 2025, https://www.youtube.com/live/sMhAmJGGV-w, accessed 28 June 2025.

[5] Pope Leo XIV, "Address of His Holiness Pope Leo XIV to the College of Cardinals," May 10, 2025, https://www.vatican.va/content/leo-xiv/en/speeches/2025/may/documents/20250510-collegio-cardinalizio.html, accessed 28 June 2025.

[6] Holy See Press Office, "Meeting with the College of Cardinals, 10.05.2025" (May 10, 2025), https://press.vatican.va/content/salastampa/en/bollettino/pubblico/2025/05/10/250510a.html, accessed 28 June 2025.

[7] Pope Francis, "Apostolic Exhortation *Evangelii Gaudium*," November 24, 2013, https://www.vatican.va/content/francesco/en/apost_exhortations/documents/papa-francesco_esortazione-ap_20131124_evangelii-gaudium.html, accessed 28 June 2025.

[8] Pope Leo XIV, "Address of His Holiness Pope Leo XIV to the College of Cardinals."

[9] Baptist World Alliance and Catholic Church, *The Word of God in the Life of the Church: A Report of International Conversations Between the Catholic Church and the Baptist World Alliance, 2006-2010* (Falls Church, VA: Baptist World Alliance, 2013), §§ 156-58, https://baptistworld.org/wp-content/uploads/2021/01/Baptist-Catholic-Dialogue-Phase-II.pdf, accessed 28 June 2025.

[10] Deborah Castellano Lubov, "Pope Leo XIV prays at tomb of late Pope Francis at St. Mary Major," *Vatican News* (May 10, 2025), https://www.vaticannews.va/en/pope/news/2025-05/pope-leo-xiv-prays-mary-and-before-francis-santa-maria-maggiore.html, accessed 28 June 2025; *Vatican Media*, 10-05-2025 Visita Santa Maria Maggiore, 02371_10052025, https://photo.vaticanmedia.va/it/10-05-2025VisitaSantaMariaMaggiore/4546404-0237110052025.html, accessed 28 June 2025.

[11] Pope Leo XIV, "Homily of the Holy Father Leo XIV in the Crypt of Saint Peter's Basilica," May 11, 2025, https://www.vatican.va/content/leo-xiv/en/homilies/2025/documents/20250511-messa-grotte-vaticane.html, accessed 28 June 2025.

[12] Pope Leo XIV, "Regina Caeli," May 11, 2025, https://www.vatican.va/content/leo-xiv/en/angelus/2025/documents/20250511-regina-caeli.html, accessed 28 June 2025.

[13] Anna Sieges Beal, Facebook post, June 12, 2025, https://www.facebook.com/share/p/1LMsLcjXTa/, accessed 28 June 2025.

[14] Steven R. Harmon, "Le sfide per il nuovo papa: L'elezione del cardinale Prevost, papa Leone XIV, seguita nella Sala stampa del Vaticano da un teologo battista americano," trans. Marta D'Auria, *Riforma* 33, no. 20 (May 13, 2025), pp. 1 and 16, https://riforma.it/2025/05/13/le-sfide-per-il-nuovo-papa/, accessed 28 June 2025.

Chapter 10
A Theology for Journalists (and Everyone Who Uses Words)

On the morning of Monday, May 12, journalists in Rome who were accredited by the Holy See Press Office for covering the funeral of Pope Francis, the papal conclave, and the beginnings of the pontificate of Pope Leo XIV were granted an audience with the new pope in the Paul VI Audience Hall adjacent to St. Peter's Basilica. Incidentally, but in my own thinking symbolically, this structure had recently been the main venue for sessions of the Synod on Synodality.

I was joined there by fellow Good Faith Media contributor Grace Ji-Sun Kim, a Korean-Canadian theologian serving on the faculty of Earlham School of Religion in Richmond, Indiana, who was passing back through Rome following a conference in Assisi related to an ecumenical initiative to add a feast focusing on creation, or God the Creator, to the liturgical calendar. She was granted temporary accreditation by the Holy See Press Office to write about the audience from her perspective as a Presbyterian theologian.[1] While we waited for the audience to begin, we discussed our perspectives on the outcome of the conclave, our impressions of Pope Leo XIV thus far, our anticipation of the audience with journalists, and our thoughts about the significance of the papacy for our respective Baptist and Presbyterian communions. We recorded part of our conversation for Good Faith Media and made plans for a follow-up recorded conversation after the audience.[2]

Shortly after 11:00 a.m., Pope Leo XIV, clad in white alb, sans cape or stole, accompanied by caretaker of the papal household Bishop Leonardo

Sapienza, who wore a black cassock and red sash, along with another similarly-attired member of the curia, was smiling and waving to us as he strode past members of the Swiss Guard to take his seat in the center of the front platform of the audience hall. The event was not a press conference, but an opportunity for the new pope to address members of the media, thank us for our coverage of the events of the past few days, and share with us his own thoughts about the roles and responsibilities of journalists.

I was deeply moved by this last aspect of his address to us, which occupied the bulk of his remarks. In my opinion, this was the most deeply theologically substantive thing Pope Leo communicated publicly in the first five days of his papacy—and each address, homily, and message up to that point had been infused with theological substance. He outlined a Christian theological framework for the practice of journalism, with implications for anyone who uses words to communicate.

This is what he said:

Address of the Holy Father Leo XIV to Representatives of the Media

Good morning and thank you for this wonderful reception! They say when they clap at the beginning it does not matter much, if you are still awake at the end and you still want to applaud…thank you very much!

Brothers and sisters,
I welcome you, representatives of the media from around the world. Thank you for the work you have done and continue to do in these days, which is truly a time of grace for the Church.

In the Sermon on the Mount, Jesus proclaimed: "Blessed are the peacemakers" (Mt 5:9). This is a Beatitude that challenges all of us, but it is particularly relevant to you, calling each one of you to strive for a different kind of communication, one that does not seek consensus at all costs, does not use aggressive words, does not follow the culture of competition and never separates the search for truth from the love with which we must humbly seek it. Peace begins with each one of us: in the way we look at others, listen to others and speak about others. In this sense, the way we communicate is of fundamental importance: we must say "no" to the war of words and images, we must reject the paradigm of war.

Let me, therefore, reiterate today the Church's solidarity with journalists who are imprisoned for seeking to report the truth, and with these words I also ask for the release of these imprisoned journalists. The Church recognizes in these witnesses—I am thinking of those who report on war even at the cost of their lives—the courage of those who defend dignity, justice and the right of people to be informed, because only informed individuals can make free choices. The suffering of these imprisoned journalists challenges the conscience of nations and the international community, calling on all of us to safeguard the precious gift of free speech and of the press.

Thank you, dear friends, for your service to the truth. You have been in Rome these past few weeks to report on the Church, its diversity and, at the same time, its unity. You were present during the liturgies of Holy Week and then reported on the sorrow felt over the death of Pope Francis, which nevertheless took place in the light of Easter. That same Easter faith drew us into the spirit of the Conclave, during which you worked long and tiring days. Yet, even on this occasion, you managed to recount the beauty of Christ's love that unites and makes us one people, guided by the Good Shepherd.

We are living in times that are both difficult to navigate and to recount. They present a challenge for all of us but it is one that we should not run away from. On the contrary, they demand that each one of us, in our different roles and services, never give in to mediocrity. The Church must face the challenges posed by the times. In the same way, communication and journalism do not exist outside of time and history. Saint Augustine reminds of this when he said, "Let us live well and the times will be good. We are the times" (*Discourse* 80.8).

Thank you, therefore, for what you have done to move beyond stereotypes and clichés through which we often interpret Christian life and the life of the Church itself. Thank you because you have captured the essence of who we are and conveyed it to the whole world through every form of media possible.

Today, one of the most important challenges is to promote communication that can bring us out of the "Tower of Babel" in which we sometimes find ourselves, out of the confusion of loveless languages that are often ideological or partisan. Therefore, your service, with the words you use and the style you adopt, is crucial. As you know, communication is not only the transmission of information, but it is also the creation of a culture, of human and digital environments that become spaces for dialogue and discussion. In looking at how technology is developing, this mission becomes ever more necessary. I am thinking in particular of artificial intelligence, with its immense potential, which nevertheless requires responsibility and discernment in order to ensure that it can be used for the good of all, so that it can benefit all of humanity. This responsibility concerns everyone in proportion to his or her age and role in society.

Dear friends, we will get to know each other better over time. We have experienced—we can say together—truly special days. We have shared them through every form of media: TV, radio, internet, and social media. I sincerely hope that each of us can say that these days unveiled a little bit of the mystery of our humanity and left us with a desire for love and peace. For this reason, I repeat to you today the invitation made by Pope Francis in his message for this year's World Day of Social Communications: let us disarm communication of all prejudice and resentment, fanaticism and even hatred; let us free it from aggression. We do not need loud, forceful communication, but rather communication that is capable of listening and of gathering the voices of the weak who have no voice. Let us disarm words and we will help to disarm the world. Disarmed and disarming communication allows us to share a different view of the world and to act in a manner consistent with our human dignity.

You are at the forefront of reporting on conflicts and aspirations for peace, on situations of injustice and poverty, and on the silent work of so many people striving to create a better world. For this reason, I ask you to choose consciously and courageously the path of communication in favor of peace.

Thank you all and may God bless you![3]

While except for the opening paragraph it was delivered in Italian, the phrasing of the English version that scrolled on video screens in the hall and was later provided online suggests that it was first composed in English and translated into Italian—and, of course, the new pope's first language is English. When I followed it on screen during delivery and again when I subsequently read more closely the online English version, I was grateful for Leo's appreciation for the work journalists do and its importance to society, and for his recognition of the dangers faced by journalists whose work in the service of the human flourishing—which is God's goal for humanity—is a threat to those who threaten human flourishing.

A Challenge to Do Things with Words, Responsibly

As a theologian, I was deeply impressed by how Leo's brief address functioned as a theology of journalism. The Christian theological ethicist Stanley Hauerwas has proposed that the task of theology is to help us do things with words.[4] Leo helps journalists be responsible in how they do things with words first by reminding us that words do in fact do things, and by impressing upon us that the things that words do are theologically significant.

Communication occurs within a world for which God's intention is *shalom*, the peace of the reign of God, all creation in right relationship. When sin—that which is contrary to God's intentions for the world—enters the picture, the result is alienation rather than relationship and community, with violence as its enduring symptom. Our words are not neutral participants in this world. They can foster community, or they can fracture community.

Leo told those of us whose vocation is the careful use of words that we must attend to the responsibility that comes with this vocation, for it addresses both things that are at the heart of God's intentions for the world and things in the world that are opposed to these intentions. The stakes of the responsibility to use words to further the peace of the reign of God were underscored by the setting of Leo's address in front of Pericle Fazzini's haunting bronze sculpture *La Resurrezione*, which depicts the resurrected Christ rising from the devastation of nuclear war.

Once again, Pope Leo mentioned artificial intelligence as a potential threat to the flourishing God intends for humanity, this time insisting that everyone, "in proportion to his or her age or role in society," has the responsibility to ensure that this developing technology serves the common good. When he characterized communication as "not only the transmission of information, but…also the creation of a culture, of human and digital environments that become spaces for dialogue and discussion," it occurred to me that Leo may become the pope who most fully attends to what the Vatican II Decree on the Media of Social Communications *Inter Mirifica* gestured toward, without knowing what the media of social communications that we now know as today's "social media" would become half a century later.[5] Apparently I wasn't the only one making this connection. When I shared Good Faith Media's publication of my article on the audience with journalists to Facebook, one of my former students commented, without knowing I had the same thought, "I'm going to go back and read the whole document, but if memory serves, his is vibing (as they say these days) this lesser-known document from the Second Vatican Council," linking to *Inter Mirifica* on the Vatican web site.

And once again, Leo employed the memorable "disarmed and disarming" phrase that appeared in his initial words to the world as Pope Leo XIV on Thursday, May 8: "Disarmed and disarming communication allows us to share a different view of the world and to act in a manner consistent with our human dignity." I predict that future historians are going to remember this language in association with this pontificate.

There is a sense in which the vocation of every person involves the use of communication to seek the peace of the reign of God. Pope Leo's invitation to journalists to participate in the reign of God through their use of words was an invitation to all of us to do so.

A Memorable Exit

Following the conclusion of his address to us, Pope Leo greeted individually select journalists who had been seated at the front of the audience hall.

We were able to see, but not hear, these interactions thanks to the large video screens in the hall, and it appeared that Leo was listening earnestly to each person's greetings and responding to each in a warm, personal manner. His longest conversation was with NBC Nightly News anchor Lester Holt, who featured his recounting of the off-mic conversation in that evening's broadcast.[6] I had enjoyed meeting Holt as we waited in the security line for the audience earlier that morning, which fulfilled one of my wife's expressed wishes for my time in Rome. Knowing that I would likely be working in proximity to some well-known journalists, Kheresa had said, "If you see Lester Holt, you have to meet him and take a picture with him." I'd been looking out for him for the past eight days to no avail, but when I arrived at the security line that morning, I immediately recognized the tallest, best-dressed man there as Lester Holt. He graciously obliged Kheresa's request.

We had assumed that Pope Leo would exit the audience hall the same way he entered it, via the side of the central platform. But when he concluded his final individual conversation with the journalists at the front, he seemed to make a spur-of-the-moment decision to walk up the central aisle to the back of the hall, greeting and shaking hands with people on the aisle along the way with attendants and guards following him. The rest of us who had been seated neither at the front nor on the aisle thronged toward the back of the room, hoping to be closer to him as he exited. Grace and I both found ourselves climbing over a railing to move closer, but alas, the pope had already disappeared through the crowd out of the hall.

In the audience hall, Grace and I met up with Cathleen Falsani, who was there to cover the papal inaugural Mass that upcoming Sunday along with Chicago connections to the new pope for the *Chicago Sun-Times*, and headed to lunch at Il Wine Bar De' Penitenzieri, where we were joined by Ernest Bonaventure Ogbonnia Okonkwo, professor of canon law at the Pontifical Urbanian University in Rome, who was Grace's host during her time in the city. Cathleen and I are both longtime fans of the rock band U2, and during lunch we were talking about how Pope Leo's decision to exit through the crowd up the central aisle reminded us of Bono's efforts to make personal connections with concertgoers by occasionally jumping off the stage to wade into the crowd. It seems that this will be a pope who, though an introverted personality, will be intentional about actions that make embodied connections with people.

NOTES

[1] Grace Ji-Sun Kim, "Witnessing History: A Presbyterian at the Vatican," *Good Faith Media* (May 12, 2025), https://goodfaithmedia.org/witnessing-history-a-presbyterian-at-the-vatican/, accessed 30 June 2025.

[2] Good Faith Media (@gfmediaorg), "Enjoy this behind-the-scenes moment with Steve Harmon and Grace Ji-Sun Kim," Instagram, May 13, 2025, https://www.instagram.com/reel/DJmzvVXurOE/, accessed 30 June 2025; idem, "Steve Harmon and Grace Ji-Sun Kim react and respond to what they saw and heard at the Pope's address to journalists," Instagram, May 14, 2025, https://www.instagram.com/reel/DJpprwTOP8H/, accessed 30 June 2025.

[3] Pope Leo XIV, "Address of the Holy Father Leo XIV to Representatives of the Media," May 12, 2025, https://www.vatican.va/content/leo-xiv/en/speeches/2025/may/documents/20250512-media.html, accessed 28 June 2025.

[4] Stanley Hauerwas, *Working with Words: On Learning to Speak Christian* (Eugene, OR: Cascade Books, 2011).

[5] Second Vatican Council, *Inter Mirifica* ("Decree on the Media of Social Communications," December 4, 1963, https://www.vatican.va/archive/hist_councils/ii_vatican_council/documents/vat-ii_decree_19631204_inter-mirifica_en.html, accessed 29 June 2025.

[6] NBC News, "Lester Holt speaks with Pope Leo," YouTube, May 12, 2025, https://youtu.be/Q9SOGL7J1no?feature=shared, accessed 30 June 2025.

Chapter 11
Baptists and the Pope

On Sunday, May 18, Pope Leo XIV was formally inaugurated in a Mass in St. Peter's Square. The whole church beyond the Catholic Church participated in the inauguration of his ministry, represented by ecumenical guests that included leaders of the Eastern Orthodox Churches, the Churches of the East such as the Coptic Church and the Syrian Orthodox Church, the World Council of Churches, and the Christian world communions from the Anglican Communion to the World Pentecostal Fellowship.

I had returned home from Rome on Wednesday, May 14. But the global Baptist community was represented in the Mass, as Baptist World Alliance General Secretary Elijah Brown was among the leaders of Christian world communions who participated. Brown's very presence in St. Peter's Square for this occasion was a sign of substantial ecumenical progress in the relationship between Baptists and the Bishop of Rome. By the time the Bishop of Rome finished the homily he preached during the Mass, he had implicitly recognized the global Baptist community in a subtle but theologically significant way that could open up the possibility of further ecumenical progress.

Baptist Responses to Pope Leo XIV's Election

There had already been other Baptist recognitions of the significance of the election of the pope for the whole church beyond the Catholic Church. Some leaders of Baptist communions and organizations released statements responding to the news of the election of Cardinal Robert Prevost as Pope Leo XIV. Less than four hours after the new pope was presented to the public on the central balcony of St. Peter's Basilica on May 8, Paul Baxley, Executive Coordinator of the Cooperative Baptist Fellowship, issued this statement:

> Today I invite all Cooperative Baptists to join Christians all over the world in praying for Pope Leo XIV as he begins his leadership of the Roman Catholic Church.
>
> Let us pray that the Holy Spirit guides him, and the Church he leads, to even greater faithfulness for the sake of Christ and the world. Let us join with him, our brothers and sisters in the Catholic Church, and with Christians from every denomination and every land in experiencing and extending the peace of the Risen Christ, offering compassion to those who suffer, and advocating for a just and peaceful end to the conflicts that plague our world.
>
> Just before his death and resurrection, Jesus prayed that all of his followers in every time and place would be one. While there is certainly difference and distinction in the body of Christ, and certainly between Baptists and Catholics, we can be one in our participation in the mission of Christ, in the work of bringing good news to the poor, release to the captives, recovery of sight to the blind and freedom for the oppressed.
>
> As the new Pope declared today: "We are disciples of Christ. Christ goes before us. The world needs His light. Humanity needs Him as the bridge to be reached by God and His love."[1]

Also on May 8, National Baptist Convention USA, Inc. President Boise Kimber released a letter offering congratulations and prayer:

> It is with heartfelt joy and deep admiration that I extend my warmest congratulations on the historic election of Pope Leo XIV, the [267th] Pope of the Roman Catholic Church and the first American to ascend to the papacy. This moment marks a significant chapter not only in the history of the Catholic Church but also in the broader landscape of global Christianity.
>
> His elevation is a powerful testament to the universality of the Church and a beacon of hope for believers across the world. In a

time of profound social, moral, and spiritual complexity, his leadership promises a renewed voice of compassion, justice, and reconciliation. May his service be marked by the wisdom of the Holy Spirit, the humility of Christ, and the courage to speak truth in love.

I celebrate this milestone with Pope Leo XIV and pray for his strength, protection, and success in the sacred responsibility entrusted to him. May God continue to use him as an instrument of peace and a shepherd of God's people across all nations.[2]

BWA General Secretary Brown sent a letter addressed to Pope Leo XIV dated May 12, but it was not released publicly.[3] The statements/letters from the Cooperative Baptist Fellowship, the National Baptist Convention USA, Inc., and the Baptist World Alliance are the only responses from Baptist ecclesial communions of which I am aware from the days following the conclusion of the conclave.

While not an ecclesial communion, the Baptist Joint Committee for Religious Liberty, an organization dedicated to advancing historic Baptist commitments to protecting religious liberty and defending the separation of church and state, on May 8 posted on social media a statement from Executive Director Amanda Tyler honoring "the significance of today's papal election for the Catholic Church and its global community" but underscoring the global nature of Christianity in contrast to nationalism, seemingly guarding against any triumphalist response of Christians in the United States to the election of a pope from their country.[4]

Some Baptist pastors issued statements for the membership of the churches they serve. For example, Ryon Price, Senior Pastor of Broadway Baptist Church in Fort Worth, Texas, devoted his weekly letter to the congregation on the day following the papal election to expressing his appreciation for ecumenical encounters with Catholic friends and for the ministry of Pope Francis along with his hopes and prayers for the ministry of Pope Leo.[5]

A much larger number of Baptist denominational groups had issued public statements in response to the news of the death of Pope Francis on April 21. Among them was the Baptist World Alliance, which issued a statement from General Secretary Brown that was posted to the BWA Facebook page, accompanied by a photograph of the members of the joint commission for the Baptist-Catholic international ecumenical dialogue with Pope Francis on the occasion of a private audience with him during the final meeting of Phase III of the dialogue in Rome in December 2022.[6] While there were many positive affirmations of this statement expressed in the comments, there were also numerous vitriolic denunciations of the BWA statement in the comment thread, accusing the BWA, among other things, of consorting with the Antichrist.

Evolving Baptist Perspectives on the Papacy

Identification of the pope with the Antichrist is unfortunately not a recent novel development in the Baptist tradition. An early Baptist confession of faith, the *Second London Confession* (1670/1688/1689), identified the pope as the Antichrist.[7] Dispensationalist eschatologies that later became popular with some Baptists sometimes identified the pope as a leader of a false worldwide religion supposedly prophesied by the book of Revelation.

The discredited approach to Baptist historiography known as "Landmarkism" regarded Baptists as the only true expression of the church of Jesus Christ through the centuries and was especially averse to acknowledging any sort of legitimacy of either the office of the pope or of the Catholic Church led by him. Many Southern Baptist missionaries to Latin American countries in the late nineteenth and early twentieth centuries were influenced by Landmarkist perspectives, shaping the strong anti-Catholic perspectives that have marked some expressions of Baptist life in Latin America.

When leaders of some Latin American Baptist unions reacted strongly against the Baptist World Alliance's approval of the agreed report of a first phase international ecumenical dialogue between the BWA and the Catholic Church that took place from 1984 through 1988, an uncharacteristic hiatus in the dialogue ensued that lasted until 2006, when the dialogue resumed with Phase II (2006–2010) and then Phase III (2017–2022).

The report from Phase II of the Baptist-Catholic dialogue included a substantial section that addressed Baptist and Catholic perspectives on "The Ministry of Oversight and Unity in the Life of the Church." It noted that "For their part, most contemporary Baptists wish to disassociate themselves from harsh names applied to the papacy by their ancestors in very different circumstances," thus disavowing the "Antichrist" language applied to the papacy earlier in the Baptist tradition.[8]

The report also included a Baptist affirmation of positive contributions of the office of the pope that benefit Baptists and other non-Catholic Christians. It pointed out:

> The witness of recent popes to many truths and values of the Gospel which are also cherished by the Baptist community has prompted many Baptist church leaders and scholars to re-evaluate long-cultivated views of the papacy ... Many Baptists can acknowledge some practical advantages to having a voice that can speak at times for the whole of the Christian community. This can serve a prophetic function, especially by drawing upon Scripture and proclaiming in our day the perennial truths of Christian faith. The usefulness of such teaching for catechesis and social solidarity extends more broadly than to the Catholic Church alone, so showing features of a ministry of unity.[9]

"A Certain, though Imperfect, Communion"

I was thinking about this evolution in Baptist perspectives on the papacy while seated in the Paul VI Audience Hall adjacent to St. Peter's Basilica awaiting our journalists' audience with Pope Leo XIV on May 12 along with fellow Good Faith Media contributor Grace Ji-Sun Kim, who is a Presbyterian theologian. While waiting for the new pope to arrive, we discussed our understandings of the significance of the papacy from the perspectives of our respective ecclesial communions.

I told Grace that as a Baptist, I belong to a non-hierarchical denomination in which the highest level of the church is the local congregation as the decision-making body within the body of Christ. We don't have a pope, but the pope is nonetheless significant for Baptists. No other figure in worldwide Christianity has the opportunity to be a spokesperson, a voice on behalf of the church—speaking for the church and speaking truth to the world prophetically.

I also applied to Baptists what the documents of the Second Vatican Council—in particular, its "Decree on Ecumenism" (*Unitatis Redintegratio*)

—say about us. We are "separated brothers and sisters" who are in a "certain, though imperfect, communion" with the Bishop of Rome.[10] So, the Catholic Church believes that Grace and I and other non-Catholic Christians are in communion with the Bishop of Rome. It's an imperfect communion, but it's a certain communion. And I want to live into that Catholic recognition that my fellow Baptists and I share degrees of communion with the church that has the pope as its lead bishop. In some sense Leo also functions as my bishop, even my pope, even though we don't have the same formal ecclesiastical structures. In addition, no other Christian leader in the world has the opportunity to speak in a representative manner for so many Christians worldwide and to be heard by so many people worldwide as the pope. If for no other reason than that, it should matter to Baptists who it is that is chosen to lead the Catholic Church as pope.

"Sister Christian Churches"

It's one thing for me to venture a qualified recognition of the office of the papacy as an individual Baptist ecumenical theologian. But it's a much more significant thing for the pope to do what at the beginning of this chapter I suggested that Pope Leo XIV did in his inaugural Mass homily—namely, implicitly offer a theologically-significant recognition of the status of Baptist communities of followers of Jesus Christ.

The whole homily encouraged me about the promise of this new pontificate, with Leo's emphasis on continuity with the ministry of Pope Francis, a synodal vision for the church as a community that walks together "on the path of God's love," and his call for the church to eschew worldly ways of wielding power, instead "loving as Jesus loved."

But I was particularly moved by this paragraph of the homily:

> In this our time, we still see too much discord, too many wounds caused by hatred, violence, prejudice, the fear of difference, and an economic paradigm that exploits the Earth's resources and marginalizes the poorest. For our part, we want to be a small leaven of unity, communion and fraternity within the world. We want to say to the world, with humility and joy: Look to Christ! Come closer to him! Welcome his word that enlightens and consoles! Listen to his

offer of love and become his one family: in the one Christ, we are one. This is the path to follow together, among ourselves but also with our sister Christian churches, with those who follow other religious paths, with those who are searching for God, with all women and men of good will, in order to build a new world where peace reigns![11]

As an ecumenist, I was of course attracted to the ecumenical vision expressed here of a synodal path that listens to Christ's offer of love, leading to becoming one family. "In the one Christ, we are one"—this is a reiteration of Leo's papal motto drawn from Augustine as the ecclesial and ecumenical goal of his papacy. And I appreciated the insistence on a unity that does not erase diversity: "We are called to offer God's love to everyone, in order to achieve that unity which does not cancel out differences but values the personal history of each person and the social and religious culture of every people."[12]

But this specific language brought tears of gratitude to my eyes: "This is the path to follow together, among ourselves but also with our sister Christian churches …"[13]

"Sister *churches*." Leo's use of "churches" here may not seem remarkable at all. But that is most definitely not the term that Catholic ecclesiology heretofore has applied to Baptist congregations or those of most other non-Catholic denominations. Even in the more ecumenically open perspectives of the Second Vatican Council, "church" is a term reserved only for the Catholic Church and ecclesiologically-similar churches, in particular the Eastern Orthodox churches. Other traditions are called not "churches" but rather "ecclesial communities." They do partake of important qualities of "churches," and thus they are "ecclesial." But they are not "churches" in the way that the Catholic Church understands church. Thus, they are "communities" rather than "churches." (The technical distinctions between these terms were explained more fully in Chapter 6 of this book.)

Judging from his public addresses thus far, Pope Leo XIV is not a pope who employs superfluous words or uses them carelessly. I believe it is possible that just as he sent a clear signal to those who had ears to hear when he employed the single word "synodal" in his initial address upon his election as pope, so Leo this Sunday was sending a clear signal to the non-Catholic and non-Orthodox ecumenical guests seated before him and to the ecclesial communions they represented with his deliberate use of "churches."

I think it is possible that the pope may have been communicating to Elijah Brown and the members of the Baptist World Alliance whom he represents that our churches are indeed churches and not merely ecclesial communities.

Just to make sure I wasn't basing this on an English mistranslation of the Italian in which Leo delivered the homily, I checked the Italian text—which, it turns out, says precisely the same thing but in Italian: "con le Chiese cristiane sorelle," "with the sister Christian churches."[14]

On the other hand, the published text of Leo's remarks delivered the next morning on Monday, May 18, to the "representatives of other Churches and Ecclesial Communities, as well as of other religions" who had participated in Sunday's inaugural Mass, with BWA Secretary Brown again among them, employed the standard Catholic terminology differentiating between "churches" that embody the Catholic Church's distinctive understanding of what it means to be fully church and "ecclesial communities" that embody important aspects of this understanding of church, but less than fully so.[15] (When the ecumenical guests were able to speak to Pope Leo individually after his address to them, Brown presented Leo with a painting by a ten-year-old Ukrainian girl displaced by the war, shared with him the Baptist commitment to work for peace in Ukraine, and asked him to remember all children displaced by war.[16]) It may simply be that because the event had already been planned, calendared, and publicized in advance using the technically proper ecclesiological terminology in Catholic perspective, the greeting in the first sentence of the address simply followed suit.

Yet, the omission in Sunday's homily of the "ecclesial communities" language, leaving only "sister Christian churches" (intra-Christian) and "other religious paths" (inter-religious) as the categories that referred to the guests to whom Leo directed these remarks, seems deliberate and potentially of great significance.

A Baptist Experience of Renewal

The time from the death of Pope Francis to my presence in Rome during the preparations for the conclave, the conclave itself, the election of Pope Leo XIV, and the first days of his pontificate was a deep experience of personal spiritual renewal for me as a Baptist minister, theologian, and ecumenist. It has rekindled my desire to become more fully catholic—not Catholic, upper-case C, but catholic, lower-case c, in the sense of living more fully into the fullness of the church that is "whole" (the Greek word *katholikē* literally means "according to the whole"). Leo's life and message thus far has encouraged me to seek to follow Jesus Christ more faithfully as a Baptist along with other members of the whole church, including the Catholic Church and its papal leader, on the synodal path that leads toward the "new world where peace reigns."[17] The experience has renewed my commitment to my vocation as a Baptist ecumenical theologian, which involves helping Baptists to receive the ecclesial gifts that the Catholic Church as well as other Christian traditions have that can help Baptist churches become more faithful followers of Jesus Christ, even while helping Catholics and other Christians to recognize the distinctive gifts that are present in the Baptist tradition that can be resources for the renewal of their own churches. I hope that the ministry of Pope Leo XIV can be an encouragement to Baptists, Catholics, and all other Christians in recognizing, exchanging, and receiving these gifts.

Notes

[1] Leah Tripp, "Statement from CBF Executive Coordinator Paul Baxley on the election of a new Pope," CBF Blog (May 8, 2025), https://cbf.net/statement-from-cbf-executive-coordinator-paul-baxley-on-the-election-of-a-new-pope/, accessed 30 June 2025.

[2] National Baptist Convention, USA, Inc., "From the Office of the President: We celebrate this milestone with Pope Leo XIV," Facebook, May 8, 2025, https://www.facebook.com/nationalbaptistconvention/posts/pfbid02PvYJM3VdJVQbkcLkTM6YiW2BPLRvm1nXknfCyubufEbnqvJvw8FcLLYDWvvVwBVKl?rdid=655MXhN0bnPcKBue, accessed 30 June 2025.

[3] Elijah Brown, e-mail message to Steven R. Harmon, May 12, 2025.

[4] BJC—Baptist Joint Committee for Religious Liberty, "Statement from Amanda Tyler, Executive Director of BJC," Facebook, May 8, 2025, https://www.facebook.com/ReligiousLiberty/posts/pfbid025vpZBrQpPkEbeeUtx3FKkKf8sPtnNYQv8McmE3WocWoZwwpzD9EZDXGoZo5Tk7TFl?rdid=oW0FwG8C4qvPYIzh#, accessed 30 June 2025.

[5] Ryon Price, "My Friday Letter," Facebook, May 9, 2025, https://www.facebook.com/ryon.price.5/posts/pfbid0pChP8havyKPdJedcRE5XqCyvjKU8HscHwPU2negU3Uz2BQAFuAPV1bDvahY45NwBl?rdid=jXc6GUxZQkWvBfrO#, accessed 30 June 2025.

⁶ Baptist World Alliance, "Today the global Baptist family joins with the world in remembering the life and legacy of Pope Francis," Facebook, April 21, 2025, https://www.facebook.com/BaptistWorld/posts/pfbid0ctTFrsPCQ8xPfp35coTzbKPh5KzHLXndSs31Pp3t4TTacYECi8A4s2MCFQDuFZoGl?rdid=m5hDiDjqZtt9UJcx#, accessed 30 June 2025.

⁷ *Second London Confession* 26.4, in *Baptist Confessions of Faith*, 2nd rev. ed., ed. William L. Lumpkin and Bill J. Leonard (Valley Forge, PA: Judson Press, 2011), 284.

⁸ Baptist World Alliance and Catholic Church, *The Word of God in the Life of the Church: A Report of International Conversations Between the Catholic Church and the Baptist World Alliance, 2006-2010* (Falls Church, VA: Baptist World Alliance, 2013), § 201, https://baptistworld.org/wp-content/uploads/2021/01/Baptist-Catholic-Dialogue-Phase-II.pdf, accessed 30 June 2025.

⁹ Ibid., § 203.

¹⁰ Second Vatican Council, *Unitatis Redintegratio* (Decree on Ecumenism), November 21, 1964, § 3, https://www.vatican.va/archive/hist_councils/ii_vatican_council/documents/vat-ii_decree_19641121_unitatis-redintegratio_en.html, accessed 30 June 2025.

¹¹ Pope Leo XIV, "Homily of the Holy Father Leo XIV," May 18, 2025, https://www.vatican.va/content/leo-xiv/en/homilies/2025/documents/20250518-inizio-pontificato.html, accessed 1 July 2025.

¹² Ibid.

¹³ Ibid.

¹⁴ Pope Leo XIV, "Omelia del Santo Padre Leone XIV," May 19, 2025, https://www.vatican.va/content/leo-xiv/it/homilies/2025/documents/20250518-inizio-pontificato.html, accessed 1 July 2025.

¹⁵ Pope Leo XIV, "Address Of The Holy Father to Representatives of Other Churches and Ecclesial Communities," May 19, 2025, https://www.vatican.va/content/leo-xiv/en/speeches/2025/may/documents/20250519-altre-religioni.html, accessed 1 July 2025.

¹⁶ Elijah Brown, text message to Steven R. Harmon, May 19, 2025.

¹⁷ Pope Leo XIV, "Homily," May 18, 2025.

CHAPTER 12
WHAT'S AHEAD FOR LEO XIV'S PONTIFICATE?

"May you live in interesting times!" is often quoted as an ancient Chinese saying that could function either as a blessing or a curse. Its actual origins are probably Western and more recent rather than Chinese and ancient, but Leo XIV has certainly become pope at a most interesting time that represents both challenges and opportunities for the new pontificate.

What are these challenges/opportunities? This chapter begins by identifying some challenges that are primarily (but not exclusively) intra-Catholic and then moves toward those that are more universal.

SOLIDIFYING SYNODALITY

One of the big questions going into the conclave was whether the cardinal electors would choose a pope who would continue Pope Francis' commitment to "synodality," an understanding of the church as a community in which all its members are "walking together on the path," with a commitment to listening to the voices and experiences of all the members of the church (and not only Catholics) and a less-hierarchical inclusion of non-ordained persons in positions of leadership, even as heads of departments within the structure of the Vatican. The goal of this listening is not merely to take into consideration a wide variety of viewpoints, but to discern the voice of the Spirit of God speaking through these diverse voices.

The cardinals' selection of their fellow cardinal Robert Prevost removed any doubts as to where the cardinals stood on Francis' synodal vision for the church. The commitment to synodality voiced by Prevost when he spoke in the pre-conclave daily congregations of the cardinals reportedly played a key role in his emergence as the preference of the cardinals, and he invoked the term in his address when presented to the public as the new pope—and he has continued to do so.

But the work of the Synod on Synodality is not yet finished. While in the hospital in March 2025 before his death, Francis approved its continuation through an additional three-year process of implementing the conclusions and proposals of the Synod, culminating in an Ecclesial Assembly in October 2028. Whatever the outcoming of this next phase of the process may be, it will fall to Pope Leo to advocate for its reception at all levels of the church. If the ongoing reception of the reforms of the Second Vatican Council is any indication, the reception of this work on synodalilty will not happen all at once and will encounter resistance. Six decades after Vatican II, some Catholics romanticize pre-Vatican II Catholicism, and that seems to be something of a trend among young candidates for the priesthood in the United States.

Intra-Catholic Division

Speaking of Catholic differences on synodality and the reforms of the Second Vatican Council in which synodality is rooted: Pope Leo XIV will begin his papacy in the context of pushback by some Catholics against the papacy of Pope Francis, whose legacy the new pope has pledged to carry forward in his own papacy. He understands the dynamics and threat of what has been called the "Alt-Catholic" movement, particularly in the United States. Soon after the election of Cardinal Robert Prevost as pope, a Catholic friend called my attention to the fact that as head of the Vatican's Dicastery of Bishops, then-Cardinal Prevost was directly involved in dealing with the case of former Tyler, Texas, Bishop Joseph Strickland, whose frequent outspoken criticism of Pope Francis approached the level of dissident status.[1] An investigation by the Dicastery for Bishops under Prevost's leadership led to the conclusion that his continued service in the office of bishop was not feasible and recommended that he resign. Two days after Strickland refused to resign, Pope Francis removed him as bishop on November 11, 2023. Much of the opposition to the papacy of Pope Francis was based in the United States, so it may prove to be significant that a pope from the

United States who is most definitely not associated with this opposition has succeeded Francis.

Pope Leo will also lead a Catholic Church that, like many other churches, is not all of one mind about LGBTQ+ issues. Shortly before I departed from Rome on Wednesday, May 14, I received a message from one of my former divinity students, who asked, "Any thoughts on where the pope falls on LGBTQ+ issues?" I replied, "My sense is that there won't be much difference in overall stance on LGBTQ+ issues between Francis and Leo. Francis still maintained official church teaching on same-sex relationships and expressed some suspicion about 'gender ideology' beyond the traditional binary, yet in tone and practice was much more open and inclusive while not making any changes to official church teaching. I do think it's probable that Leo XIV will perhaps be more careful/precise in his expressions in this area than Francis, but I don't expect the overall stance of welcome to all to change."

On *America* magazine's Inside the Vatican podcast, which I listened to daily from the death of Pope Francis through my time in Rome covering the conclave and beginning of the new pontificate, veteran Vatican journalist Gerard O'Connell observed that Francis' more open approach was consistent with his formation as a member of the Jesuit religious order, which tends to be theologically comfortable with raising questions, proposing some possible answers, and being patient with an ongoing dialogue between the questions and the biblical and traditional sources of the faith which may suggest how the questions and answers may best be framed today.[2]

It will be interesting to see how Pope Leo's background as an expert in Catholic canon law may shape how he approaches this and others matters under contestation by Catholics today. One of my lunch companions after Pope Leo's audience with journalists on May 12 was Ernest Bonaventure Ogbonnia Okonkwo, a professor of canon law at the Pontifical Urbanian University in Rome. The new pope earned a doctorate in canon law from the Pontifical University of St. Thomas Aquinas in Rome (also known as the "Angelicum)" and was a professor of canon law, patristics, and moral theology at a seminary in Peru for a decade. I asked my new friend over lunch how that background might influence Leo's pontificate. He replied that he thought it would make him perhaps more "careful" than Francis in his manner of expression when replying to questions about controversial matters. I will be watching closely to see how this might play out in the future. I am eagerly anticipating Pope Leo XIV's first encyclical, which I imagine might combine the theological precision of Pope Benedict XVI with the pastoral sensitivity and open engagement of Pope Francis.

Another matter of intra-Catholic division that has people wondering how Pope Leo XIV might be positioned in relation to it is liberation theology and its legacy. Liberation theology maintains that in circumstances of oppression, God sides with the oppressed and seeks their liberation, and the responsibility of the church as the people of God is to join God in liberating people from oppression. One influential stream of liberation theology originated in conferences of Latin American bishops that in the late 1960s recognized the church's failures in confronting oppressive regimes in many contexts in Central and South America. The most influential articulation of this emerging movement happened to be a book by a Peruvian Catholic theologian: Gustavo Guitérrez's *A Theology of Liberation*, published in Spanish in 1971 and in English translation in 1973.[3] Since Prevost was working in Peru while Gutiérrez was active in Peru, this raises the question: what was Prevost's relationship to Gutiérrez? An article in the Madrid newspaper *El País* published on May 9 addressed this question and noted that "during his time in Peru, he maintained a good relationship with Gustavo Gutiérrez, the father of Liberation Theology."[4]

Pope Benedict XVI had been notably critical of liberation theology, especially prior to his pontificate when Ratzinger was head of what was then the Congregation for the Doctrine of the Faith. Pope Francis was regarded as much friendlier to the emphases of liberation theology. The specifics of how Pope Leo XIV will relate to the movement's concerns remain to be seen, but multiple contemporary Latin American liberation theologians interviewed for a July 1 article in the *National Catholic Reporter*, including the influential Brazilian liberation theologian Leonardo Boff, expressed optimism that Leo would follow in the footsteps of Pope Francis and even prove to be a "cheerleader for liberation theology," in the words of the article's author summarizing the liberation theologians' comments.[5]

Clergy Sexual Abuse

No pope can ignore the scandal of clergy sexual abuse in the Catholic Church. No Christian tradition is untouched by the great damage done to people by sexual abuse perpetrated by members of the clergy; my own Baptist tradition is having its own ongoing reckoning with it. But public attention worldwide has been especially focused on the Catholic Church's response to revelations of sexual abuse, and that church's sheer size and global presence amplify the scale of public awareness.

On the one hand, Pope Leo's relationship with American Catholicism means that he is very much aware both of the coverage of the scandal by North American media and, positively, of the concrete steps taken to implement safeguards against abuse in Catholic parishes in the United States. Two days before the conclave began, the *National Catholic Reporter* published an opinion piece by Anne Barrett Doyle, co-director of BishopAccountability.org—an organization that researches cases involving the abuse of children by priests and members of religious orders and how those cases have been managed by bishops, religious orders and the Holy See—which was titled, "Why the Next Pope Should Be an American." She noted, "Thanks largely to the United States' unique civil justice system and robust free press, bishops here have been forced to adopt more prudent policies on abuse than bishops in any other country have."[6] Barrett Doyle argued that the Catholic Church would be best positioned for dealing with sexual abuse and attempts to cover it up if it were to adopt universally the U.S. bishops' policies of zero tolerance (removing from ministry those convicted of abusing a minor) and public disclosure. After the election of Leo XIV, she told *America* magazine that she did not have Prevost specifically in mind when she wrote the op-ed but hoped that "he's absorbed enough of the American sensibility around zero tolerance and around disclosure, too, that he might apply those practices in addressing abuse in the global church."[7]

On the other hand, there had been reports of dissatisfaction with the handling of allegations of abuse in the diocese where then-Bishop Prevost served in Peru. These cases were related to a Catholic society in Peru, the Sodalitium Christianae Vitae (SCV). Since Pope Leo's election, however, more information has been reported regarding Prevost's communications with victims of abusers connected with the SCV and his efforts to get the allegations addressed, with several survivors crediting him with actions that were eventually taken. When Prevost became prefect of the Dicastery for Bishops, investigators from the Vatican were sent to Peru, leading to the expulsion of fourteen members of the SCV and the resignation of the Archbishop of Lima eight years short of his normal retirement age.[8] With Leo's emphasis in his address to journalists on the power of communication both to harm and to heal,[9] I cannot imagine that he will refrain from addressing this issue publicly and with intentionality in his pontificate. And in light of his previous responsibilities for the discipline of bishops throughout the Catholic Church as head of the Dicastery for Bishops, surely his attention to this issue will not only be concerned about what the Catholic Church says about clergy sexual abuse, but also about what the Church does about it.

On June 20, Pope Leo sent a message to be read aloud publicly at a performance of a play in Lima, Peru, that is based on the work of Peruvian investigative journalist Paola Ugaz, who had reported on abuse by members of the SCV and who had exchanged greetings personally with Leo when she attended the audience with journalists in Rome on May 12. In the letter, Leo praised the work of journalists in bringing abuse to light so that there may be accountability, called the Church to the "conversion" necessary to follow a "path of humility, truth, and reparation," and pledged a "commitment to guarantee the protection of minors and vulnerable adults." He also noted in the message that "Wherever a journalist is silenced, the democratic soul of a country is weakened."[10]

ECUMENICAL RELATIONSHIPS

As the center of unity for Catholic Christians, the pope also has responsibility as a focal point of ecumenical relationships between the Catholic Church and other Christian churches, as Pope John Paul II recognized and addressed in his 1995 encyclical "On Commitment to Ecumenism" (*Ut Unum Sint*).[11] Soon after his election, it was reported that Pope Leo XIV would make the first scheduled international trip of his papacy to ancient Nicaea, now Iznik in Turkey. Pope Francis and Eastern Orthodox Ecumenical Patriarch Bartholomew had planned together an ecumenical celebration of the 1700th anniversary of the First Ecumenical Council of Nicaea on

May 26 in Turkey, and Francis had planned to attend. (The Council of Nicaea opened in May 325 and concluded in August of that year.) As of the writing of this book, official details about when the visit to commemorate the First Ecumenical Council would take place were not yet confirmed, but there were reports of indications that it would take place in late November 2025, probably in connection with the Feast of St. Andrew on November 30.

Ecumenical Patriarch Bartholomew had attended the funeral of Pope Francis. Bartholomew and Leo met in Rome in connection with the May 18 papal inaugural Mass and had a conversation during the audience with ecumenical and interreligious guests on the following day, during which they discussed the possibility of the visit to Turkey, and they met again for a private audience on May 30 when Bartholomew was in Rome to receive the Laudato Si' Award from the Order of Friars Minor along with Brazilian liberation theologian Leonardo Boff in recognition of their ecological advocacy.[12]

These ecumenical encounters between pope and patriarch and their plans for commemorating the 1700th anniversary of the Council of Nicaea together have immediate implications for the continuation of the great progress that has been made since the Second Vatican Council on working through the issues that have divided the Catholic Church and the Eastern Orthodox Churches since their schism in the year 1054. But since the decisions of the Council of Nicaea regarding Trinitarian theology and Christology are in some sense the doctrinal heritage of all Christians, the participation of Pope Leo in this celebration has implications for ecumenical relationship beyond those with the Eastern Orthodox churches, which Leo himself has noted. On June 7, Pope Leo addressed a symposium on "Nicaea and the Church of the Third Millennium: Towards Catholic-Orthodox Unity" sponsored by the Institute for Ecumenical Studies of the Angelicum. (It's worth noting in this connection that the Angelicum, the Pontifical University of St. Thomas Aquinas where Pope Leo earned both a licentiate—equivalent to an advanced master's degree—and a doctorate in canon law, is the only Catholic university in Rome with an ecumenical institute.) In his remarks to the symposium, Leo noted that the Trinitarian faith of Nicaea is the shared faith not only of Catholicism and Orthodoxy but of all Christians. He reiterated his commitment to the goal of the full visible unity of all Christians and suggested that the Council of Nicaea in 325 was a precedent for a "synodal path" of theological dialogue between Christians divided from one another. He said, "I am convinced that by returning to the Council of Nicaea and drawing together from this common source, we will be able to see in a different light the points that still separate us" and "gain a better understanding of the mystery that unites us."[13]

In the days after the conclave, I wondered what the new pope's record of ecumenical relationships while serving as a bishop in Peru might have been. On the day before I departed Rome, I stopped by the offices of the Dicastery for Promoting Christian Unity to meet with Monsignor Juan Usma Gómez, head of the Western Section of the Dicastery. Msgr. Juan is the Catholic Co-Secretary for the commission to the Baptist-Catholic dialogue, Phase III, for which I am the Baptist Co-Secretary, and we met principally to discuss next steps in the process of finalizing and seeking official approval by our respective communions of the report from the dialogue. But since Msgr. Juan is originally from Colombia, during our conversation I asked him what he knew about Prevost's ecumenical relationships while serving in Peru. He told me that in Peru, the ecumenical divisions are principally between Catholics and evangelicals broadly construed. He said that a friend in Peru with close knowledge of these dynamics had told him that as bishop, Prevost had a positive record of relating warmly to evangelical leaders there.

There is something explicitly ecumenical embedded in the papal motto Pope Leo XIV has drawn from Augustine: In *Illo uno unum*, "In the One, we are one," from Augustine's *Exposition on Psalm 127*: "although we Christians are many, in the one Christ we are one."[14] As an ecumenical theologian interested especially in Baptist-Catholic dialogue, I will be watching closely the ecumenical dimensions of this pontificate.

GEOPOLITICS

In the first few days of his pontificate, Pope Leo XIV mentioned peace as God's desire for humanity and referenced specific conflicts that contravene God's peace multiple times in virtually every public address. His first words to the world when introduced as the new pope on the central balcony of St. Peter's Basilica on May 8 were "Peace be with you all!"[15] repeated in his first post from the papal social media accounts on Tuesday, May 13.[16] He mentioned in particular the Russia-Ukraine, Israel-Palestine, and India-Pakistan conflicts in these first addresses.

On Wednesday, May 14, Leo met with representatives of the twenty-three Eastern rite churches that are in full communion with Rome. He noted that many of them had come from places in the Middle East and Eastern Europe where violent conflicts are raging. He said, "Rising up from this horror, from the slaughter of so many young people, which ought to provoke outrage because lives are being sacrificed in the name of military conquest, there resounds an appeal" for the end of war, saying that he is voicing this as an appeal "not so much of the Pope, but of Christ Himself, who repeats, 'Peace be with you!' Let us pray for this peace, which is reconciliation, forgiveness, and the courage to turn the page and start anew."[17]

He then pledged the willingness of the Holy See "to help bring enemies together, face to face, to talk to one another ... so that peoples everywhere may find hope and recover ... the dignity of peace."[18] In the days before the opening of the papal conclave, some observers had speculated that in light of the current geopolitical challenges, the cardinals might seek to elect a pope with diplomatic experience and skills. While that has not been part of the new pope's previous portfolio, it seems that he is committed to playing a role in facilitating peace among nations.

In addition to various wars and what Pope Leo has characterized as an emerging "piecemeal third world war,"[19] the geopolitical context of the beginning of his papacy includes a growing attraction in many countries to populist authoritarian movements and figures that threaten democracy. Leo has been acquainted with such movements firsthand, both as a bishop in Peru, where people have periodically experienced authoritarian regimes, and as a citizen of the United States, where we have been experiencing our own increasingly authoritarian presidential administration. It may be that Pope Leo XIV is uniquely situated for addressing this particular geopolitical threat.

AMERICA

And speaking of political developments in the United States: it is hugely significant that at this particular moment, the new pope has an insider's experience of the American political system and its current travails. He has participated in the American political system as a voter, and not in a way that necessarily places him at a particular point on our political spectrum. As several reports have documented, Robert Prevost had voted in many primary and general elections with a registered address in Illinois, which is an open primary state in which voters may choose in which party primary they will vote in a particular year. Sometimes Prevost voted in the Republican primary; sometimes he voted in the Democratic primary. We do not know how he voted in general elections; we know that he voted in the November 2024 presidential election by absentee ballot from Rome.

The new pope can identify with the common American experience of negotiating life in a politically-divided family. One of his brothers has indicated having more liberal political leanings; another brother has expressed much more conservative political views. And it appears that he may even have had the experience of contending about politics with family members over social media. From a personal Facebook account that has since been taken offline, a Robert Prevost who was a Facebook friend of Robert's sister-in-law (the wife of the more conservative Prevost brother) in the weeks before the 2024 presidential election had replied to a post by the sister-in-law that had passed along a false allegation about Democratic candidate Kamala Harris in a comment that fact-checked the post with a link to a Snopes article debunking it.[20]

I speculate that before his election as the successor of Pope Francis, the new pope had already closely advised Francis on how to respond to some of these American political challenges. The last theologically significant document issued by Francis before his death was his February 10 "Letter of the Holy Father Francis to the Bishops of the United States of America" that denounced the Trump administration's efforts at mass deportation and implicitly but directly rejected the appeal of Catholic Vice President JD Vance to the Augustinian concept of an *ordo amoris*, a "hierarchy" or "ordering" of loves, as a religious justification for directing one's energies and resources to meeting the needs of our own nation rather than caring for migrants and refugees from other nations who come to our nation. Francis had written, "The true *ordo amoris* that must be promoted is that which we discover by meditating constantly on the parable of the 'Good Samaritan'…that is, by meditating on the love that builds a fraternity open to all, without exception."[21]

Prevost had been brought to Rome by Francis in 2023 to serve as head of the Dicastery for Bishops. I imagine that Francis would have leaned upon this trusted cardinal from the United States for advice about how to respond to Trump's executive orders and Vance's defense of them by appealing to Augustine. Furthermore, Prevost did not merely belong to the Augustinian religious order. As Pope Leo XIV he selected a quotation from Augustine as his papal motto, and his public addresses since becoming pope have included multiple quotations from Augustine. I suspect that the then-future Pope Leo helped Pope Francis craft this response, and I think this may foreshadow a papacy with unique opportunities for constructive engagement of a disarrayed American political order.

We should not underestimate the impact that having a pope whose first language is not only English, but American English, will have on the reception of papal communications in the United States. Modern popes have had varying degrees of facility with English as one of many secondary languages in which they have tried to communicate, but their more limited capacity for doing so had the effect of making the papacy seem more remote to speakers of English. With Pope Leo that is no longer the case, and it will be interesting to watch how this may influence how both American Catholics and the American public at large respond to the pontificate of Leo XIV.

CLIMATE

Pope Leo XIV succeeds a pope who will long be remembered as an ecologically aware pope for his direct theological engagement of the climate crisis. His first solo-authored encyclical "On Care for Our Common Home" (*Laudato Si*) has been credited with influencing the outcome of the 2016 Paris Climate Agreement.[22] Leo begins his pontificate at a time when many nations, and his native United States in particular, have been backpedaling from and in some cases formally disengaging from the Paris Agreement.

Pope Leo has signaled a clear commitment to Francis' ecological perspectives on the reality of climate change and the urgency of reducing carbon emissions. According to the *National Catholic Reporter*, in June 2017, when President Trump was considering withdrawing the United States from the Paris Climate Agreement, Robert Prevost's Twitter account retweeted a post from the Laudato Si' Movement urging Trump to read Francis' *Laudato Si'* encyclical.[23] Signaling that the climate crisis is on the agenda of his pontificate, on June 16 Leo said to bishops from Madagascar who were in Rome for their Jubilee pilgrimage, after mentioning the beauty of Madagascar, "Take care of creation, which groans in pain, and teach your faithful the art of protecting it with justice and peace"[24]

TECHNOLOGY

Pope Leo XIV has directly linked his choice of a papal name to the manner in which his predecessor Leo XIII had responded to the late nineteenth century industrial revolution and its adverse impact on humanity. In this connection he has identified the emergence of new technologies, in particular artificial intelligence, as potential threats to human dignity and the dignity of work. It is clear that he has long been thinking about A.I. theologically, and I would not be surprised at all if the first encyclical of his papacy directly addresses it. In any case, as a professor of theology and Christian ethics, I am eagerly awaiting the release of that initial encyclical, which may well address multiple issues mentioned in this chapter as challenges his pontificate will face.

NOTES

[1] The Pillar (joint staff byline), "Pope Francis meets to discuss Strickland resignation," *The Pillar* (September 11, 2023), https://www.pillarcatholic.com/p/pope-francis-meets-to-discuss-strickland, accessed 1 July 2025.

[2] American Media, *Inside the Vatican*, April 29, "Clarity, Confusion, Unity: Unpacking the conclave's code words," https://podcasts.apple.com/us/podcast/clarity-confusion-unity-unpacking-the-conclaves-code/id1439165420?i=1000705424366, accessed 1 July 2025.

[3] Gustavo Gutiérrez, *Teología de la liberación* (Liima: CEP, 1971); idem, *A Theology of Liberation: History, Politics, and Salvation*, trans. and ed. Caridad Inda and John Eagelson (Maryknoll, NY: Orbis Books, 1973).

[4] Íñigo Domínguez, "Leo XIV: The first pope from the United States, a figure in the spirit of Francis," *El País* (May 9, 2025), https://english.elpais.com/international/2025-05-09/leo-xiv-the-first-pope-from-the-united-states-a-figure-in-the-spirit-of-francis.html, accessed 1 July 2025.

[5] Eduardo Campos Lima, "Liberation theologians in Latin America express hope for Pope Leo," *National Catholic Reporter* (July 1, 2025), https://www.ncronline.org/news/liberation-theologians-latin-america-express-hope-pope-leo, accessed 1 July 2025.

⁶ Anne Barrett Doyle, "Why the next pope should be an American," *National Catholic Reporter* (May 5, 2025), https://www.ncronline.org/opinion/guest-voices/why-next-pope-should-be-american, accessed 2 July 2025.

⁷ Colleen Dulle, "How will Pope Leo tackle the sex abuse crisis?" *America* (June 12, 2025), https://www.americamagazine.org/faith/2025/06/12/pope-leo-sex-abuse-rupnik-250908, accessed July 2, 2025.

⁸ Stefano Pozzebon, Christopher Lamb, Caitlin Stephen Hu, and David von Blohn, "How Pope Leo dealt with years of abuse allegations in a powerful Catholic society in Peru," CNN, May 18, 2025, https://www.cnn.com/2025/05/18/americas/pope-leo-peru-sodalitium-intl-latam, accessed 1 July 2025.

⁹ Pope Leo XIV, "Address of the Holy Father Leo XIV to Representatives of the Media," May 12, 2025, https://www.vatican.va/content/leo-xiv/en/speeches/2025/may/documents/20250512-media.html, accessed 28 June 2025.

¹⁰ Christopher Lamb, "Pope Leo praises work of journalists in first public comments on clerical abuse scandal," CNN, June 21, 2025, https://www.cnn.com/2025/06/21/europe/pope-leo-church-abuse-scandal-message-intl?Date=20250621&Profile=cnn&utm_content=1750508260&utm_medium=social&utm_source=threads, accessed 1 July 2025; Salvatore Cernuzio, "Pope urges Church to foster a culture that does not tolerate abuse," *Vatican News* (June 21, 2025), https://www.vaticannews.va/en/pope/news/2025-06/pope-leo-xiv-abuse-zero-tollerance-church-message-peru.html, accessed 1 July 2025.

¹¹ Pope John Paul II, *Ut Unum Sint* (On Commitment to Ecumenism), May 25, 1995, https://www.vatican.va/content/john-paul-ii/en/encyclicals/documents/hf_jp-ii_enc_25051995_ut-unum-sint.html, accessed 1 July 2025.

¹² Gabriel López Santamaría, "Ecumenical Patriarch Bartholomew I receives the Laudato Si' Award," *Vatican News* (May 31, 2025), https://www.vaticannews.va/en/church/news/2025-05/ecumenical-patriarch-bartholomew-i-receives-laudato-si-award.html, accessed 2 July 2025.

¹³ Gerard O'Connell, "Pope Leo on Nicaea, synodality and a common date for Easter," *America* (June 7, 2025), https://www.americamagazine.org/faith/2025/06/07/pope-leo-xiv-nicaea-ecumenism-common-date-easter-250878, accessed 2 July 2025.

¹⁴ Saint Augustine, *Expositions of the Psalms, Vol. 6, Ps 121-150*, trans. Maria Boulding, in *The Works of Saint Augustine: A Translation for the 21st Century*, ed. Boniface Ramsey (Hyde Park, NY: New City Press, 2004), 100–101.

¹⁵ Pope Leo XIV, "First Blessing 'Urbi et Orbi' of His Holiness Pope Leo XIV," May 8, 2025, https://www.vatican.va/content/leo-xiv/en/messages/urbi/documents/20250508-prima-benedizione-urbietorbi.html, accessed 28 June 2025.

¹⁶ Pope Leo XIV (@pontifex), "Peace be with you all!" Instagram, May 13, 2025, https://www.instagram.com/p/DJmOVZAiFXQ/, accessed 2 July 2025.

¹⁷ Christopher Wells, "Pope Leo XIV to Eastern Catholics: The Church needs you," *Vatican News* (May 14, 2025), https://www.vaticannews.va/en/pope/news/2025-05/pope-leo-xiv-to-eastern-catholics-the-church-needs-you.html, accessed 2 July 2025.

¹⁸ Ibid.

¹⁹ Pope Leo XIV, "Regina Caeli," May 11, 2025, https://www.vatican.va/content/leo-xiv/en/angelus/2025/documents/20250511-regina-caeli.html, accessed 28 June 2025.

²⁰ Mark Shea, "Another consolation: Our Holy Father knows the pain of American Catholics who have lost friends and family to the MAGA Cult and of trying to bring them back to sanity," Facebook, May 9, 2025, https://www.facebook.com/mark.shea2/posts/pfbid0jcSZYtd664SiuogGq

bcVVcFWi7PagY7dGCKWfUurdVQDhATXHy8n2YwwCgettXA4l?rdid=HkgYIksDgewudzcT#, accessed 2 July 2025.

[21] Pope Francis, "Letter of the Holy Father Francis to the Bishops of the United States of America," February 10, 2025, https://www.vatican.va/content/francesco/en/letters/2025/documents/20250210-lettera-vescovi-usa.html, accessed 2 July 2025..

[22] Pope Francis, "Letter of the Holy Father Francis to the Bishops of the United States of America," February 10, 2025, https://www.vatican.va/content/francesco/en/letters/2025/documents/20250210-lettera-vescovi-usa.html, accessed 2 July 2025.

[23] Brian Roewe, "Before he was pope, Leo XIV said it's time for action on climate change," National Catholic Reporter (May 9, 2025), https://www.ncronline.org/earthbeat/he-was-pope-leo-xiv-said-its-time-action-climate-change, accessed 2 July 2025.

[24] Devin Watkins, "Pope Leo XIV: Bishops must not turn gaze from the poor," *Vatican News* (June 16, 2025), https://www.vaticannews.va/en/pope/news/2025-06/pope-leo-xiv-madagascar-bishops-jubilee-pilgrimage-audience.html, accessed 2 July 2025.

Chapter 13
A Prayer for Pope Leo XIV

Two weeks after my return from Rome, I traveled to Dayton, Ohio, for the annual convention of the College Theology Society, an academic organization of Catholic scholars who teach the theological disciplines in universities, at the University of Dayton. Since 1997, a "Region at Large" of the National Association of Baptist Professors of Religion has met jointly with the annual conventions of the College Theology Society. This has been an important influence on my formation as a Baptist ecumenical theologian, and a few years ago I published a history of this Baptist-Catholic scholarly ecumenical collaboration.[1]

I had been invited to make a presentation in a special panel session, "*Habemus Papam!* Initial Thoughts on Pope Leo XIV," along with Lucas Briola (Saint Vincent College, Latrobe, Pennsylvania), Neomi DeAnda (University of Dayton, Dayton, Ohio), and Julie Rubio (Jesuit School of Theology of Santa Clara University, Berkeley, California), convened by Jason King (St. Mary's University, San Antonio, Texas). We were invited to share our own hopes for the new pontificate. This is what I shared:

A Baptist's Hopes for Pope Leo XIV

My day job is theology professor, but my introduction to Pope Leo XIV came while moonlighting as a journalist. I was in Rome as a special correspondent for Baptist-related Good Faith Media to cover the conclave, along with the last couple of days of the cardinals' pre-conclave daily congregations and the first few days of the new pontificate.

However, I was not a disinterested journalist. As a Baptist ecumenical theologian serving as co-secretary for the Baptist-Catholic dialogue joint commission, I'm keenly interested in how the pope, whomever he may be, might live into the hope that the papacy could be of service to all Christians, articulated by John Paul II in *Ut Unum Sint*[2] and reiterated last year in the Dicastery for Promoting Christian Unity study document on *The Bishop of Rome*.[3]

There are two ways to frame Baptist identity in relation to the whole church. Both have roots in the journey of John Smyth, co-founder of the first Baptist congregation in 1609 in Amsterdam. He sought to establish his community as a true church, and not finding any other communities that qualified as such from which he and his co-religionists might receive a true baptism, Smyth baptized himself and then the other members of his church. But a year later he concluded that the local Mennonite fellowship was in fact a true church and sought to join it along with a portion of his congregation. While some Baptists have regarded other Christian traditions as lacking the marks of the true church, as Smyth initially thought, many others have followed his subsequent re-thinking in recognizing the authenticity of church wherever it may be found.

In this latter perspective, the Baptist movement is a renewal movement within the one church of Jesus Christ with a charism of ecclesial freedom in covenanted local community—not unlike religious orders following a distinctive rule for their life together. My Baptist hopes for the pontificate of Pope Leo XIV are related to his connections with various renewal movements within the one church.

Monasticism originated as just such a renewal movement, and I find Leo's Augustinian identity that has permeated his early addresses promising for a papacy that serves as an instrument of ecclesial renewal, not only for the Catholic Church but for all churches. His explicit embrace of Pope Francis' vision of a more fully synodal church seems connected to an Augustinian emphasis on the virtue of listening for the voice of God in the voices of the community. As the Synod on Synodality's conferences on synodality in different Christian traditions demonstrated, there are practices of synodality in other churches, Baptists among them. The Baptist practice of ecclesial discernment by listening to the voices of the whole local congregation is one such practice, and in its ideal exercise it seeks to listen to a wide range of voices beyond the local church. I hope that Pope Leo will inspire all Christians toward church-renewing practices of deep listening through modeling the listening that several cardinal electors reportedly recognized as one of his strengths.

The missionary movement has contributed much to the renewal of the church across its history. Baptist participation in the modern missions movement has deeply influenced Baptist identity. The Catholic Church was of course a missionary church long before the modern missions movement. But Pope Leo's background as a missionary priest, seminary professor, and bishop in Peru positions him well for leading the church to heed his summons in his initial *Urbi et Orbi* message to be a missionary church. I hope his leadership will renew the missional commitment of the whole church that includes Baptists.

The modern ecumenical movement that sprang initially from the modern missions movement has likewise been a source of renewal for the churches. Pope Leo has related his papal motto, "In the One, we are one," to his concern for the ecumenical renewal of the whole church. I'm trying to resist the temptation to read too much ecclesiological precision into Leo's reference to "sister Christian churches" rather than "ecclesial communities" in his inaugural mass homily with the guest ecumenical representatives seated before him. But I was nonetheless deeply moved by this language, and I hope it anticipates an ecumenically engaged papacy.

I think the American identity of this pope has potential for the renewal of American Christianity in particular by calling us beyond our captivity to a polarized politics toward a fuller participation in the reconciling peace of the reign of God. He has already inspired me to strive to resist positioning myself in relation to the polarized categories of American civil as well as ecclesial life.

This Baptist is hopeful that the pontificate of Pope Leo XIV contributes to the renewal of the one church of Jesus Christ in each of these ways, and more.[4]

A Baptist's Prayer for Pope Leo XIV

Two weeks before the College Theology Society annual convention in Dayton, I was wrapping up my time in Rome and preparing to travel home. On my final evening in Rome, I enjoyed one final dinner at Il Wine Bar De' Penitenzieri. While I waited for my meal, I wrote out a prayer that I wanted to pray for Pope Leo XIV before leaving the city. Ever since Pope Francis asked the members of the joint commission for our Baptist-Catholic dialogue to pray for him in the first words he spoke to us when we met him at the end of a general audience in December 2018, I've tried to pray for the pope whenever he has crossed my mind. I wanted the future prayers I'll be praying for his successor to be rooted in a recollection of the space where he was elected and first presented to the public.

After dinner I walked to the spot in St. Peter's Square at the back end of the left colonnade where, on the evening before the papal conclave began, I had stood and prayed for God's Spirit to guide the cardinals in discerning whom they should elect as the successor to Pope Francis.

This time as I looked across the square toward St. Peter's Basilica, I prayed for the ministry of the one whom the cardinals had elected. Here is what I prayed for Pope Leo:

> Gracious and merciful God,
> By your grace and in your mercy
> you have given to your very human church
> very human leadership,
> that we might walk together
> on the road that leads to what you intend for all creation.
> Thank you for giving the Catholic Church
> and the whole church
> your servant Pope Leo XIV

as one of these gifts of leadership.
Thank you for everyone in his journey
who has recognized in him gifts for ministry and encouraged him in his calling.
Thank you for the people and experiences who have prepared him for this new task:
his family and friends,
his priests and teachers;
his life experiences of all sorts
and the experiences of others
that have helped him understand the human condition;
the Rule of St. Augustine that has shaped his spiritual discipline,
and his life together with Augustinian brothers lived in covenant relationship;
his students, parishioners, and fellow ministers in Peru;
the priests and bishops he supervised,
and the cardinals with whom he has sought to discern the way your church should go.
Thank you for Pope Leo XIII, for Pope Francis,
and for others who have helped him imagine
how he might lead the church of today.
By your Spirit, give him the strength, love, wisdom, courage, grace, love of justice, mercy, and humility he needs
to lead your church
and to encourage your world
toward the peace of your reign.
Deepen his devotion to Christ and his way,
That he might continue to grow in faith and faithfulness.
Help him to continue listening deeply to the voices of other people,
and to discern your voice in their voices.
Help him to lead your world away from violence
and toward peace.
Help him truly to be a "bridge-builder,"
building bridges between communities of followers of Christ divided from one another,

bridges between nations at war with one another,
bridges between people alienated from one another,
bridges between people and creation itself,
for our common life demands that we cross these bridges.
Help us to be faithful in praying for your servant Leo,
and help us to discern your voice in his voice
and take it to heart and live it out in our lives,
Through Jesus Christ our Lord,
who lives and reigns with you in the unity of the Holy Spirit,
one God, forever and forever. Amen.

I invite the readers of this book to join me in praying for Pope Leo in the days ahead. In the midst of circumstances in the world that sometimes tempt me toward hopelessness, I find myself daring to hope that God is doing a new thing in Pope Leo XIV that will lead the whole church to participate more fully in God's renewal of all creation. May we all heed the summons that concluded his inaugural Mass homily: "Together, as one people, as brothers and sisters, let us walk towards God and love one another."[5]

NOTES

[1] Steven R. Harmon, "The Traditioned Word in the Life of the Church: The Influence of the NABPR Region-at-Large/CTS Partnership on the Second Baptist–Catholic International Dialogue (2006–2010)," chapter in *American Catholicism in the 21st Century: Crossroads, Crisis, or Renewal?*, ed. Benjamin Peters and Nicholas Rademacher (Maryknoll, NY: Orbis Books, 2018), 177–188.

[2] Pope John Paul II, *Ut Unum Sint* (On Commitment to Ecumenism), May 25, 1995, https://www.vatican.va/content/john-paul-ii/en/encyclicals/documents/hf_jp-ii_enc_25051995_ut-unum-sint.html, accessed 1 July 2025.

[3] Dicastery for Promoting Christian Unity, *The Bishop of Rome: Primacy and Synodality in the Ecumenical Dialogues and in the Responses to the Encyclical Ut Unum Sint. A Study Document* (Collana Ut Unum Sint, no. 7; Rome: Libreria Editrice Vaticana, 2024).

[4] A published version of my contribution to the College Theology Society panel session on Pope Leo XIV appeared as part of a series essays about the election of the first pope born in the United States featuring contributions from "notable Catholics and Americans from various perspectives within the faith community" whom the *National Catholic Reporter* invited "to write about their hopes, dreams and expectations for Pope Leo XIV": Steven R. Harmon, "A Baptist theologian hopes for renewal in Pope Leo's service to all Christians," National Catholic Reporter (August 5, 2025), https://www.ncronline.org/opinion/guest-voices/baptist-theologian-hopes-renewal-pope-leos-service-all-christians, accessed 12 August 2025.

[5] Pope Leo XIV, "Homily of the Holy Father Leo XIV," May 18, 2025, https://www.vatican.va/content/leo-xiv/en/homilies/2025/documents/20250518-inizio-pontificato.html, accessed 1 July 2025.

www.ingramcontent.com/pod-product-compliance
Lightning Source LLC
Chambersburg PA
CBHW071006160426
43193CB00012B/1938